"Dallas Willard used to say that eternity is already in session. Laurie Short has written an elegant invitation to live life from inside eternity rather than on the outside."

John Ortberg, senior pastor, Menlo Church

"The true stories Laurie uses throughout this book make its message impossible to ignore. If you need your world rocked by new eyes for your current circumstances, then you need this book."

Lisa Anderson, director of Boundless.org, author of *The Dating Manifesto*

"The flourishing of our lives depends so much not only on *what,* but *how* we see. In *When Changing Nothing Changes Everything,* Laurie Short has offered us a concise, accessible guidebook that provides not only helpful instruction but—more importantly—hope for how a proper vision of the life we have can lead to the very world of goodness and beauty for which we long so deeply. Read this book—and see your life change before your very eyes."

Curt Thompson, author of *The Soul of Shame* and *Anatomy of the Soul*

"Abraham Herschel said that 'we must learn to be surprised.' Sometimes we grow so numb to how things are that we miss how things were meant to be. We lose the surprise. We lose the mystery. Laurie Short captures this idea through story beautifully and calls us to find ourselves surprised again, helping us to change everything by reframing the world we ˿

Brooklyn Lindsey, author, pastor of Somos Church, globa¹ the Justice Movement

"What matters most to me about Laurie Short be honest and faithful both to the Bible and to human. This is the converging power and insig. us, and it's why we need to hear her."

Mark Labberton, president, Fuller Theological Seminary

"Laurie Short has written a powerful and empowering book. She's proven why perspective matters, but even deeper, she's shown us we have control over the aperture of our lives. And who doesn't need a new lens on life?"

Nicole Johnson, author of *Creating Calm in the Crazy,* founder of Seasons Weekend

"I used to think changing perspective was a cop-out for not changing, but what Laurie is proposing—reframing the drama of your life—is actually the way to live fully in God's reality, which is something far bigger than our seasonal drama. I've seen how that really does change everything!"

John Burke, pastor of Gateway Church, author of *Imagine Heaven*

"*When Changing Nothing Changes Everything* speaks to the power of our own stories, and specifically to the way in which we remember, tell, and live them out. Laurie's call—to be a part of the bigger story—is a reminder of what's so vital and important in life."

Andrea Gurney, associate professor of psychology, Westmont College

"Laurie Short offers gracious and helpful insights that challenge us to greater self-awareness and deeper discipleship by suggesting we view our circumstances through alternate lenses. By reminding us about the power of our perspective, she holds out words of hope and help for the moments when life throws too much pain or challenge in our path. This is a great book for anyone who struggles to meet life's challenges—which is all of us!"

Meagan Gillan, director of women ministries, The Evangelical Covenant Church

WHEN

CHANGING

NOTHING

CHANGES

EVERYTHING

THE POWER OF
REFRAMING YOUR LIFE

Laurie Polich Short

IVP Books

An imprint of InterVarsity Press
Downers Grove, Illinois

InterVarsity Press
P.O. Box 1400, Downers Grove, IL 60515-1426
ivpress.com
email@ivpress.com

InterVarsity Press® is the book-publishing division of InterVarsity Christian Fellowship/USA®, a movement of students and faculty active on campus at hundreds of universities, colleges, and schools of nursing in the United States of America, and a member movement of the International Fellowship of Evangelical Students. For information about local and regional activities, visit intervarsity.org.

While any stories in this book are true, some names and identifying information may have been changed to protect the privacy of individuals.

Cover design: Cindy Kiple
Interior design: Jeanna Wiggins
Images: ©Chinnasorn Pangcharoen/iStockphoto

ISBN 978-0-8308-4479-1 (print)
ISBN 978-0-8308-8105-5 (digital)

Printed in the United States of America ∞

Library of Congress Cataloging-in-Publication Data
A catalog record for this book is available from the Library of Congress.

P	20	19	18	17	16	15	14	13	12	11	10	9	8	7	6	5	4	3
Y	34	33	32	31	30	29	28	27	26	25	24	23	22	21	20	19	18	

Contents

The eye is the lamp of the body.
If your eyes are healthy,
your whole body will be full of light.

MATTHEW 6:22

The Things You May Not See

remember the morning well. It was a few months after I had moved to Santa Barbara, California, and the pastor I was working for invited me to give the sermon at my church. People were still getting to know me, so I decided to start by sharing a typical scene from my life. Here's how I began:

> I got up this morning in my apartment, and I was all alone. I have no husband, so there are no kids. The owner recently put a "For Sale" sign in the front yard, so I probably won't be able to stay in my place much longer. The rent will go up, and I'll have to find something else. Dating at my age is not easy, because everyone you meet has baggage. It's just a matter of choosing what luggage you can live with. Whether it's a divorce, shared kids, or the reasons that accompany prolonged singleness, it's been impossible to find anyone I am interested in. I love it here, but working at a church is one of the hardest jobs a single person can have. You feel your singleness everywhere you go.

I paused, and an awkward silence fell across the crowd. Noticing the pastor staring at me with a look of wonderment (not the good kind), I took a deep breath and started again:

> I got up this morning and I had the whole place to myself. It was quiet, and I could do whatever I wanted. The "For Sale" sign is still in front of my place, so I'll be able to live there another month. If it sells, there's a chance I might find something even better. Dating is much easier at my age because you know yourself more. You are better equipped to make a good choice. You also have a lot more grace for the people you date because you realize that circumstances make life complicated. And my job? Working at a church is such a gift! What a blessing to have an extended family in the place where you work when there isn't one at home.

I should have stopped my sermon right there. Because this was the only part of the talk people remembered. It's been ten years since I gave that illustration, and there are still some people who remember it. Somehow it struck a chord and may have even planted the seed that caused me to write this book.

> **Where we choose to focus makes all the difference in what we see.**

Seventeenth-century philosopher Blaise Pascal accurately observed, "There is enough light for those who choose to see, and enough darkness for those who are of a contrary disposition." He wrote these words to describe a journey toward faith, but they are also true about life. Where we choose to focus makes all the difference in what we see.

I should pause here and tell you that this is not a book about putting on "rose-colored glasses" in your circumstances. It's about reframing what you see. In the chapters that follow, you will be introduced to four different lenses that will open up a multidimensional view of your life.

The *big view* lens will help you view your life from a broader perspective. The *present view* lens will help you see what you may be missing right now. The *rear view* lens will give you insight about the way you are wired. And the *higher view* lens will reveal more of what God wants you to see. Looking through these lenses, you will discover some different perspectives that could open up some uncharted vistas of your life.

As the title of my book suggests, these lenses won't change anything that is in front of you. They will simply expand the dimensions of what you see. But using them could change what happens from this point forward.

WHY WE NEED A MULTIDIMENSIONAL VIEW

Before the dawn of social media, we only dreamed of how the other half lived. Now we get to see it. And I have wondered about the effect this is having on our souls. Through the lens of select images and soundbites, everyone looks happier, prettier, thinner, and more fulfilled than they really are. Comparing these images to the unedited version of our own lives, it's not hard to imagine why many of us feel slightly depressed. A friend of mine used to say, "Don't compare what you know about yourself to what you don't know about someone else." Social media has turned his warning into an art.

There are parts of social media that I love: the ability to see pictures of family far away, and stay in touch with friends I no longer see. It's the wistful dissatisfaction that comes with it I could live without. In the olden days, we used to feel that way when we picked up a magazine or turned on the TV and saw people we could later convince ourselves "weren't really real." Now we see people we *know* are real. And they look like they are living a much better life than the one we have. What we forget is that when they look at us, they feel the same way.

Rarely do we race to the screen to post pictures of the bad date we had or the temper tantrum our child just had. But catch us in front of a sunset, dressed up to go out, or celebrating an honor roll or little league championship, and the camera is out, ready to post. Perpetuating the "perfect life" myth for all to enjoy.

Then we get off camera and live our real lives. And after viewing other people's images, we have that gnawing sense that if only we could . . . do . . . be . . . have . . . look like . . . *then* we would be happy. Something is missing. And the longer we think about it, the bigger it gets.

I remember the first time I wrote the word *vacation* in an email, and an ad for Bora Bora popped up on the margin of my screen. Immediately I visualized myself sitting in a beach chair by the ocean, sipping a drink in a coconut. Within minutes, my desk, my home, and for that matter my life, looked a lot less appealing. I'm guessing you have been there too.

Because we are confronted with an endless barrage of images bombarding us with what we need to be happy, seeing all that we have in front of us is a skill we need. That is what this book will help you do. Because when you stop to consider what you have, you are less likely to spend your life chasing things that will never be.

The promise of more, bigger, better, other, is an empty promise, and you discover that when you get it. You have only to pursue the next relationship, the new job, or the shiny car to realize when something is finally yours, it eventually becomes something you no longer hold dear. When you remember how you felt when you got those things, you more clearly recognize the value of what you have, and this helps you see through the mirages your current desires might tempt you to pursue. These can be feisty mirages because they not only lure you in to their promise of happiness, they also may cause you to abandon things you will discover you want much more when they are no longer yours.

The secret to living your best life lies largely in your ability to see all that is in front of you. That is what this book is about. I believe more of your life is determined by the way you see than you can imagine. The reframing principles in this book will help you see your life in new ways and may keep you from making a

> The secret to living your best life lies largely in your ability to see all that is in front of you.

decision that takes you somewhere you don't want to go. That is one of the reasons your vision is so important. This scene from my past illustrates why.

THE VIEW YOU DON'T WANT TO SEE

I remember the moment he took to the stage—he was something to behold. I was speaking at a conference, and single at the time. He was leading music at the conference, and he was exactly my type. Tall, dark, handsome, and subtly flirtatious. And he was married.

I can still remember the tapes rolling around in my head as we found ourselves strolling back to our rooms late at night. There was nothing inappropriate in what we did; we merely talked about life, and dreams, my sadness not being married, his wonderment at why I wasn't. He seemed taken by my thoughts and listened intently to my words, smiling and pensive at all the right times.

Married.

I held that thought directly in front of me as I committed myself to bring up his wife, his kids. "All good," he said. "Just been at it for a while." And maybe he would have written his life differently if he had the chance. As we parted, I closed my door, shut my eyes, and caught my breath. We were staying in a lodge with a few other people, all separate rooms. Minutes after we got back, I could hear him in the next room strumming his guitar. It was a large open area that had couches and tables where any of us could sit and talk and relax. I felt a rush of excitement when I heard him and reached for my door handle to enter his space. Then I paused. In the depths of my soul I knew what was simmering between us wasn't friendship. From him or for him. Yet how I tried to stifle that whisper. The still, small voice that said turning away now will be your least painful turn.

Yes, there were parts of my life still missing. But if I took another step, I could come close to losing what I had. The life of trusting and wanting, waiting and building. Knowing that if I kept moving forward it would be one flash of ecstasy. And a lifetime of regret. That I'd be giving in to the illusion of what could never be at the expense of compromising what each of us had. The ministries we loved. The marriage he had. The marriage I wanted someday. And with the view I made myself see, I stayed in my room. And I let distance clear my head.

Years later I heard he had an affair. And the uniqueness of how I felt under his gaze was put in the context of what time revealed. It was not me he wanted. It was someone other than the woman he had. Seeing the end had saved me.

Pausing to get an accurate view of what is in front of you can keep you from pursuing things that can hijack your life. It helps you recognize the allure is in the wanting, not in the thing you want. You have only to experience getting something you want—and living with it for a while—to discover it's never as good as you thought it would be. Keeping that truth in front of you saves you from pursuing something that takes you somewhere you don't want to be.

When you look at your desire with the end in sight, you can see how the path will end up. Then you can look with fresh eyes at what you have, trusting that for this moment, you have what you need. Considering the long view keeps you from being led by your longings to a place that is worse than where you are—especially since "where you are" is never a fixed point. The truth is, "where you are" may be leading you to a goodness that you cannot yet see. The difficulty you may want to escape could be part of your journey in getting there.

The ability to reframe and view yourself in the middle of your story enables you to rest in *what is*, knowing that it is part of what is taking you to *what we will be*. Things are happening in you—and to you—and if you attempt to escape your circumstances, rather than live them, you may actually abort a process that could be bringing something wonderful into your life. Considering the fullness of your story strengthens your resolve to live your current chapter well, and in so doing you may discover you are on a road to getting more than you ever could have dreamed. This book contains several stories of people who illustrate this truth.

However, in the parts of our lives that hold long periods of darkness or disillusionment, we may need help acquiring a better view of our story. From listening to people in these chapters (as well as my own life), I have observed the tendency to get fixated on what is *not* there, and even though peering through a bakery window isn't the best place to position ourselves when we feel starved, it is that view that tempts us most. During these seasons we need people around us to shift our focus and teach us to hold the things we want in their proper perspective. If we take a moment to look around us, there are people who can help us make this shift.

THOSE WHO DIRECT OUR EYES

Over a span of thirty years, several mentors in my life taught me some vision principles that helped me form the lenses that shape this book. There are times when gaining perspective from someone you trust is wise; it helps you see things more accurately.

The first mentor I had was a woman named Gini. I lived with Gini in my midtwenties, when my college degree was becoming irrelevant to my career path, and the marriage I desired was nowhere in sight. We took walks together every morning, and she started each one with a ritual I was both irritated by and drawn to, but for some reason never forgot. "Thank you for legs that walk and arms that move," she would call out to the air—and God—as we headed down the road. It felt so . . . trite. And obvious. And *of course*. Until her husband, who had MS, started to lose some of his verbal and motor skills. Suddenly, "legs that walk and arms that move," and for that matter, "voices that speak," become gifts.

I learned from Gini that I viewed many of my gifts as expectations. The only time I saw they were actually gifts was when they were taken away. One of the secrets of developing an accurate view is to train our eyes to see our gifts *before* they are taken away. Gini helped me train my eyes.

In my thirties there was Vivian. I lived with Vivian after I accepted a call to be the youth pastor at her church, and she and her husband "adopted" me as the daughter they never had. I was still single and longing to be married, and I remember envying the fact that Vivian's eyes danced when her husband entered the room. A few years later, when Vivian's husband was killed in a plane crash, she had to teach her eyes to dance for other things. Appreciating what she had, when she had it, equipped her with that ability.

Vivian taught me to live fully right "where you are," even if that is a place you don't want to be. She helped me see the joy in the good and recognize the value of the hard. Her dancing eyes in both seasons gave me that gift.

In my forties I met June. I had just ended a year and a half engagement and moved to Santa Barbara to work at Ocean Hills Church. June had a slight limp that came from a childhood bout with polio, and her mishandled illness could have paved the way to a bitter

> Live fully right "where you are," even if that is a place you don't want to be.

life. Instead, her life was anything but bitter; she managed to radiate joy to everyone she knew. The jewel June dropped into my life was to try to focus on others in the midst of unmet needs. She said, "When you feel sad, serve. By looking at others' pain, you will see your own pain differently." She was right. Unwanted singleness was my limp, and June taught me how to walk with it by putting my arms around others who limped too. By doing that, I found my limp to be less apparent.

There are others you will meet who have mentored my vision, but there is one more I must mention at the outset because of his particular influence on my perspective. He helped inspire the title of this book by showing me that it isn't necessary for your condition to change in order to live a spectacular life. You just have to embrace your life for all it can be. And you do that by living fully with all that it is.

Born to a mother who died the day after he arrived, Chris was delivered as she slipped into a coma. He weighed two and a half pounds at birth. Because he was born with no vital signs, the doctor assumed he was dead. Chris was not dead, but he had severe disabilities.

Overwhelmed with grief, Chris's dad solicited help from his in-laws, who eventually became Chris's primary caretakers. A hardworking grandfather and an overbearing grandmother proved to be a winning combination for Chris to rise above his afflictions, but it was his introduction to faith that ultimately chartered his course. After inviting God into his life, he saw what God could do with it, and he became an inspiration to others simply by the way he lived. From navigating his travel, to cooking his food, to showing up at meetings, to communicating on the phone, from speaking at schools to deejaying events, Chris's schedule continues to be filled with things you would imagine would be undoable for someone like him. And they would be for most people.

Chris shows us every day that life is not about what you have or don't have, but how you live with what you've got. His body is bound to a wheelchair, his arms work part time, and his speech is slow and (when you are not listening carefully) incoherent. Yet in spite of these disabilities, I have seen him rappel through a rainforest, race in a half marathon, and run the soundboard at our church. A couple of years ago, Chris went on his first mission trip, and he volunteered at a school in Nicaragua for disabled kids. He quickly became the hero of Nicaraguan children who thought, prior to meeting him, that they would never leave their house. If someone like Chris could make it to Nicaragua, maybe they could make it down the street. Or into school. Or maybe even try a sport. Chris did not know any Spanish when he went on the trip, but he was the only one who did not need to. He proclaimed what was possible by the way he lived his life.

Chris is a testament to what can happen when we reframe what we have and see it for what all can be. Somewhere in that process we discover it is actually *what we have* that makes our life what it is.

THE SECRET

In 2006 a book titled *The Secret* swept the *New York Times* best-seller list and made Oprah Winfrey's coveted list of must-read books. The message of the book is, *You have the power to get what you want.* Years before that, a prisoner from the New Testament wrote a letter that revealed another kind of secret: *You have the power to want what you have.*

This second "secret" audaciously proclaims that contentment can be found in any situation, right where you are. Here are the words of the prisoner's claim: "I have learned the secret of being content in any and every situation, whether well fed or hungry, whether living in plenty or in want" (Phil 4:12).

Because these words were written in a prison cell, they carry a promise that transcends all circumstances. However, one word establishes a small condition to this claim. Paul had to *learn* the secret of contentment, partly because he was in a place of discontent, and being there pressed him to see his circumstances from a broader view. By pulling back and looking at his life from a wider perspective, Paul saw more than his circumstances presented him, and this allowed him to interpret and experience his circumstances differently. With the lens of the big view, Paul saw that his current circumstances were part of a larger story, and this gave him the resolve he needed to live every chapter well. And Paul shares in the next verse that God, who gave him his story, equipped him with strength for each circumstance he faced.

Seeing the broader view of his story also enabled Paul to notice things in his immediate surroundings that he might otherwise have missed. With the present view lens, Paul was able to find purpose right where he was, because he understood that he was where he was supposed to be. Whether he was in prison to influence the prison guards, fellow prisoners, or people who would read the letters his circumstances gave him time to write, Paul understood that what was happening was a crucial part of a story that was bigger than he could see.

Paul was also able to find contentment in every situation because he had an added spiritual lens that gave him the perspective that he was where God wanted him to be. The higher view lens helped him look at each chapter of his life with God's purpose in mind and live each chapter with that conviction. Whether Paul was in plenty or in want, he found contentment in knowing that God had him there—and he trusted that God was working in him and through him in more ways than he could presently see.

By reframing his life in these ways, Paul was able to find peace and satisfaction in what was, instead of spending his days wishing for what could be. And looking back through the rear view lens added to his confidence and peace, because he could draw from God's faithfulness behind him for the course that was ahead.

In this book, you will be invited to look at your life through these four lenses. You will get a multidimensional view of your life that will broaden—and sharpen—what you see. The big view lens will help you pull back and see the breadth and power of your life. The present view lens will bring new focus to what is in front of you and help you consider the weight each moment can bring. The rear view lens will bring clarity to how your past is affecting you and build your faith for what is ahead. And the higher view lens will deepen and expand your vision to look at what God wants you to see. My hope is that through these lenses, you will learn to embrace your life—the good, the bad, the hard, and the spectacular. And with the ability to reframe your life and see all that it already is, you may start to live it differently. That's when changing nothing can change everything.

LENS 1

THE BIG VIEW

The voyage of discovery is not in seeking new landscapes but in having new eyes.

MARCEL PROUST, *THE CAPTIVE*

The Big Picture
Changes the
Small Picture

The year was 1995. I was a youth pastor at the time, and a movie was released that not only deeply inspired my calling, it had an impact on the way I viewed my life. *Mr. Holland's Opus* was the story of a high school music teacher who once dreamed of being a famous composer. Like many nonfamous artists, Mr. Holland decided to teach classes "on the side" while he waited for the career that never opened up. Because he never achieved his goals, he ended up spending thirty years occupying a job he never desired to have. However, instead of letting himself settle for a career of lethargy, best symbolized by the voice of Charlie Brown's teacher (Wah-wah-wah), Mr. Holland breathed life into his students' lives. He lived each day with passion and intention even though he was not where he had chosen to be.

Forced to retire early because of school budget problems, the last scene shows Mr. Holland quietly contemplating whether his life has been a waste. As he packs up his belongings, his wife and son arrive to lead him into the school auditorium where he is

greeted by four hundred of his former students—now adults—
who surprise him with a thunderous ovation. They have come to
pay homage to the teacher who changed their lives.

At the end of the film, Mr. Holland was able to see the big
picture of his life. It turns out it was not the goals he accomplished that made his life extraordinary—it was the way he had
lived. When he entered the auditorium, Mr. Holland discovered
that his life was part of a much bigger story, one that involved
many other lives besides his own. By getting a glimpse of the
broader impact of his life, Mr. Holland was able to see that his
greatness was not determined by how big or small his part may
have been, but by the way he played his part.

Though we are inspired by Mr. Holland, there are days when
it is easy to become Charlie Brown's teacher—particularly if our
life is not turning out the way we imagined it would be. We can
become disillusioned. Disengaged. Wah-wah-wah-ing through
our days, hoping something will happen to change the trajectory
of our life. But *Mr. Holland's Opus* reveals the important truth
that our life isn't merely shaped by the things that happen to us,
it's also shaped by the way we live. We have a bigger impact on
those around us than we may be able to see.

> What we see in front
> of us is not always
> the full picture of
> what is happening
> because of us.

What we see in front of us is
not always the full picture of
what is happening because of us.
Our lives are setting off a ripple
effect beyond what we can see.
We are not just influencing the
future of people we know, we
are also affecting the future of
people we may never know. And if we look at the stories around
us, we can see evidence everywhere of this truth.

TRACING THE SOURCE

It was September 4, 1987. The parents of Patrick and Benjamin Binder sat silently in the waiting room of a hospital in Germany, agonizing over the fate of their Siamese twins. Because their twins were joined at the skull, the only two options they faced was to lose both of their children, or sacrifice one child for the other to have a chance at life. They could not bring themselves to make that choice. Thankfully, there was a young surgeon who could imagine a different outcome. He came up with an idea to cool down the boys' bodies so the blood would flow slower and bleeding would be less severe. This would allow the surgeons to have the time to perform the delicate task of untangling, dividing, and repairing shared blood vessels.

What fueled the surgeon's imagination to come up with this idea was a choice made twenty-five years earlier by a single mother. Left alone with a third-grade education and no money, this young mother worked three jobs to help her two young boys survive. Because of this, her boys had little accountability in their studies, and both were failing in school. One night, on a rare evening at home, she suddenly knew she would have to do something drastic if she was going to alter their course. Amidst a firestorm of complaints, she told her boys that until their homework was done, they were no longer allowed to go outside and play. Any free time they had was now going to be occupied by reading two books a week at the local library and writing a summary of each book for her to see. There was only one problem with her plan: she never learned how to read.

If they had a question about a word they didn't know, she would tell them to sound it out. If during their homework they came to her for an answer to a problem, she would say, "Use your imagination." Her friends warned her that her boys would grow up resenting her, which was initially just what they did. However, in time they would say that their lives were changed because of her love. Both boys went on to achieve multiple academic successes and earn Ivy League college degrees. The older boy became an engineer. The younger boy, a pediatric neurosurgeon.

When neurosurgeon Ben Carson faced the couple sitting in the German waiting room, he heard his mother's words echoing in his brain: "Use your imagination." So that's exactly what he did. When the Binders saw their newly separated twins, they tearfully embraced their daring surgeon. What they did not know is that their children were saved in part by their surgeon's mother's sacrifice. It was the piece of the story they could not see.

History reveals that in another part of Germany, decades before, there was a single mother who did not have the strength or fortitude to do what Ben Carson's mother did. Her strong-willed son dropped out of school at the age of sixteen and left home before graduating high school. Because of the lack of authority and education in his life, as well as a volatile relationship with his father, this boy ended up gravitating toward all the wrong influences. He lived for several years in a homeless shelter, where historians say he developed many of the views that would later shape his life. As a result of a thousand small choices made by people around him, as well as choices he made himself, this boy grew up to become something very different than Ben Carson. His name was Adolf Hitler.

Our small stories play a significant part of a bigger story when we consider the impact our lives may have. We discover that each choice and sacrifice we make involves more than we can see. Certainly there are some things that will evolve in ways we can't control, but if we look through a broader lens at the people in front of us, it can give us the vision and determination we need to press on in our small sacrifices. And as Sonya Carson discovered, someday we may get a glimpse of what those sacrifices become.

BRINGING IT HOME

I am a stepmom. If it sounds like I'm introducing myself at an AA meeting, that isn't so far from how it feels. These words require work for me to own, and they don't come easily out of my mouth. After all, in the wonderful world of Disney, the stepmother is generally not the heroine of the film. The words *wicked* and *evil* come to mind when looking for adjectives to describe her.

I confess there are times when I avoid saying the word *step* before *mom* simply because the minute a woman says those words, she is announcing that she's not really the mom. She's just the fill-in when the child is staying in her home. But since Jordan's mom lives in Australia, approximately 85 percent of the time my stepson is "staying" in our home. Nevertheless, when push comes to shove in the parenting lineup, I am Mom number two.

Perhaps you have a situation in your life where the immediate view tempts you to feel insignificant in your role. Reframing your situation with the big view lens might reveal that your role is more important than you can see. If I dwell on my understudy position in Jordan's life, I am tempted to fade in the background behind my husband, because he carries the biological seed that solidifies permanence. My role feels insignificant. And the more I say that, the smaller I get.

Then I look at the power I have. As the mom Jordan is mostly exposed to, there are big things happening in our relationship—the things I say and do will help construct the man he is becoming. My words and actions have the power to put wind in his sails and to fan into flame his gifts. The deposits I make every day in his life will be part of who he becomes.

I am the face he sees when he does a speech at school. Hits a home run. Struggles with his homework. Finds vegetables hidden in his pasta. (Actually, I hide my face for that last one.) But I am a pretty big face in this growing boy's life. And however insignificant my title might make me, in the grand scheme my role could be huge in my stepson's life. Looking at it from that perspective will impact the way I live it. Perhaps looking at your situation this way will change the way you live yours.

Seeing the big picture brings a focus to our lives and enables us to see the heroic in the mundane. We recognize that every sacrifice we make, no matter how small it feels, may be setting off a chain reaction that can change another person's life. Recognizing the weight of our actions brings a significance to our lives that can inspire us to live differently. But we must see ourselves as part of something much bigger in order to live this significance out.

PART OF A BIGGER STORY

Child development studies affirm that when we are babies, the world does not exist beyond our view. When something or someone moves out of our sight, their story stops until they reenter our story. We are the focal point of all that happens and the star of every scene.

You can actually see this by observing a baby. I was watching my friend's three-month-old as her pacifier dropped onto her shoulder. It quickly became a crisis, because from her perspective the pacifier was gone. The intensity of this crisis grew with the awareness that her mother was also out of her view. When the pacifier was retrieved and her mother popped back into view, all was well again in the baby's world. These things ceased to exist for her when they were outside her limited perspective.

As we mature and our perspective changes, we become aware that life exists outside of our limited view. But if the widening of our perspective is not nurtured, we remain focused on ourselves, and the "my story" mentality becomes the lens through which we view our life. Life continues to be seen from the inside out rather than the outside in, and every relationship and circumstance we have is viewed in the context of our own story, rather than part of a bigger story that is unfolding around us.

From the "my story" viewpoint we may feel big, but our lives become small because we reduce our life to a series of scenes centered on us. Life may invite us to play a part in scenes that star other people (like my part with my stepson), but if our willingness to play those roles is determined by what we'll get from them, we may resist the opportunity. We fear we might be underappreciated or unsatisfied by the result our role may achieve. By living with this mentality, we end up living a smaller, self-focused life.

The awareness that you are a part of a bigger story helps put your life into proper perspective. Your role may feel small, but when you pull back the microscope you realize you are always involved in something bigger than you can see. The big view lens can give you the energy to play your part well no matter how small it may feel. And time occasionally reveals a glimpse of the importance of the part you played.

THE BEST WE CAN DO

The setting was World War II. The place was Berlin, Germany. After countless horrific deaths, the Allies finally began to gain ground to claim their victory. During the final months of the war, the British conducted daily bombing raids over Berlin. British Bombers would take off from an airstrip in England and fly into Germany, surrounded by smaller fighter planes whose job was to keep German planes from attacking.

One night, after a successful bombing raid, the British planes were heading back to England when they were suddenly attacked by a group of German fighter planes. One bomber found itself flying alone with no protection, and at the same time a German fighter plane appeared out of nowhere. The crew watched help-lessly as the German plane moved closer and closer, until finally it was in shooting range. They heard, "Thud! Thud! Thud! Thud! Thud!" as five bullets slammed into the fuselage of the bomber, right in the direction of the gas tank. The crew braced itself for an explosion, but after a moment of silence, they found nothing happened. Fuel was seeping from the holes in the gas tank that the bullets had made, but they were able to fly back to their base and get safely off the plane.

After the plane had landed, one of the mechanics came on board to examine what had happened. He handed the recovered bullets to the pilots, and they carefully opened each shell. To their amazement, they found four of the bullets were empty, no gun-powder inside. Inside the fifth shell they found a piece of crumpled paper wrapped into a tiny wad, which read, "We are Polish POWs—forced to make bullets in factory. When guards do not look, we do not fill with powder. It's not much but it's the best we can do."

When we reduce our life to our individual actions, it's easy to believe we are small and insignificant. But our small life quickly becomes a big life when we see the effect of our actions from a wider view. Every role we have, every circumstance we are in, every relationship we are a part of is affected by how we play our part.

Suddenly your actions matter—not only for how they will affect you but how they will affect other people. So the real question becomes, Am I willing to expand my view outside of my own story, where I am the focus, to see my part in someone else's story? To have faith that even if I cannot see the impact of my actions, time will eventually reveal their effect?

> Every role we have, every circumstance we are in, every relationship we are a part of is affected by how we play our part.

Seeing the big picture changes the small picture. But sometimes you need a reminder to look through the big view lens to see your part. There is a prayer you may have memorized that can help you do just that.

A PRAYER FOR PERSPECTIVE

In order to introduce how I first learned this prayer, I need to share a little bit of my faith history. I grew up in the Serbian Orthodox Church, which not only meant a rich cultural heritage, it also meant copious amounts of eating, drinking, and kissing. (Think *My Big Fat Greek Wedding,* only Serbian.) The kissing part included big wet ones delivered by distant aunts, as well as man-to-man ones, which had a tendency to shock newcomers. Ask my husband.

The church I grew up in had stained-glass windows, clouds of incense, and an open bar in the reception hall. As a child, I observed that a few of the adults left church early, and only later understood why. However, it was in the midst of this upbringing that a prayer was spoken at every event and church service, which stayed with me the rest of my life. When I first memorized the prayer, coming out of my mouth it sounded a little like this: OurfatherwhoartinheavenhallowedbethynameThykingdom comethywillbedoneonearthasitisinheavenGiveusthisdayour dailybreadandForgiveusourdebtsasweforgiveourdebtorsLead usnotintotemptationbutdeliverusfromevilForthineisthekingdom andpowerandgloryforever.

I knew the prayer by heart; I just did not have a clue what the prayer actually meant. But stopping to take a closer look at it, the *words* of Jesus' prayer—as well as the order in which he speaks them—directs us to the big view lens. Reciting this prayer can remind us to view our lives as part of a bigger story.

Our Father makes us aware that I am not praying to *my* God but *ours*. He's the God of the people in my home as well as the God of the person with no home, who sleeps on the streets. He's the God of families who live in Santa Barbara and the God of families who huddle in the slums of Port Au Prince. "Our Father" is more than an address, it's a jolt to our perspective. The world shares the same God, and his eyes are on us all.

Hallowed be your name acknowledges there is a power in the universe greater than ourselves. A paraphrase might be, "You are God, and I am not," which is a good reminder when we perceive ourselves as the center of the universe. All it takes is a diagnosis, a catastrophe, or tragic loss to help us realize we are not the center. The world will go on without us, and when we acknowledge God as the center, it helps us view our lives as part of a bigger story, a story that will continue after we are gone.

Your kingdom come, your will be done. If we recited this line the way most of us live, we'd say "Your kingdom come, *my* will be done," but the line as it is written invites God to adjust our will toward a greater good. "Your will be done" means I not only acknowledge a bigger story, I submit myself to be part of it. This is the Sonja Carson prayer, the one that pulls you off the couch to participate in the change you want to see. This part of the prayer moves our well-being from the focal point to God's dreams as the focal point—even if his dreams involve our sacrifice.

Finishing "Your will be done" with *on earth as it is in heaven* leaves room for God to work in ways we cannot see. It's acknowledging the higher view of our lives with the awareness that we don't always see all that's going on. When Jesus hung on the cross, no one who watched understood the scope of what was being accomplished. And on a much smaller scale, Sonja Carson couldn't see what her choice with her young boys would one day become. "Your will be done on earth as it is in heaven" is saying yes to a life bigger than you can see.

Notice we are half way through the prayer before we actually pray for something we need. This is different from the traditional concept of prayer, which often begins and ends with our needs. The first half of this prayer lines us up with God's perspective, and that causes us to see our needs differently.

Give us this day our daily bread. For the record, "Give us this day our yearly bread" would be a more comfortable prayer for me. But this line as it is written emphasizes that we are invited to ask just for what we need today. This isn't a prayer for tomorrow's bread, or for more bread than we need. It is a prayer for God's provision in the here and now. Furthermore, saying "give us" rather than "give me" nudges me to view my extra bread for tomorrow as bread someone else might need today. What I do with that perspective is directly related to whether or not I believe that tomorrow's bread for me will be resupplied.

From there we move to *forgive us our debts as we forgive our debtors.* We may wonder what this has to do with our perspective, until we stop to realize how much forgiveness affects what we say and do. The lack of forgiveness we've received impairs our ability to extend it; whereas the experience of being forgiven fuels us to live in grace. Perhaps that's why Jesus doesn't make our forgiveness the well to draw from; instead he offers God's well as the source. A paraphrase might be, "As we experience your forgiveness, help it to spill over in the way we treat others." Saying—and living—this line of the prayer could affect more people than we can imagine.

Lead us not into temptation. We know that temptation is permitted by God because all of us experience it. So "Lead us not into temptation" means asking God to help us make good choices with the freedom we have. Good gifts like food and wine and sex can become temptations when we give them too much focus in our lives. We move from enjoying them to becoming enslaved by them, and our addictions and behaviors spill onto others who might be affected by our choices.

Deliver us from evil is the prayer when we are too far in and we need the courage to see the evil our temptations have brought us. Temptation is the coworker who looks better than your spouse. Evil is the suffering your family endures when you pursue that coworker. Temptation is the Internet sex site you stumble on. Evil is the sex addiction that causes you to visit that site again and again. There is a line between temptation and evil, and here's how you find it: temptation includes your freedom; evil takes it away. Evil needs to be battled by Someone greater than us.

For yours is the kingdom and the power and the glory is a benediction that reaffirms we are here for a greater purpose than just ourselves. It gives us the perspective we need each day to see our lives as part of a bigger story. Perhaps if we recited the Lord's Prayer in words we understood, it would help us see our lives through a different lens.

> Creator of all, you see more than we can see.
> We acknowledge that you are God, and we are not.
> May you dwell inside us, so we want what you desire.
> Help us remember the world looks different from your
> 　　　vantage point than it does from ours.
> Give us just what we need today—and help us lean on
> 　　　your provision for tomorrow.
> May we experience your forgiveness so we can extend
> 　　　forgiveness to others.
> Guide us through temptation.
> Rescue us from evil.
> And help us know you hold all things—including our
> 　　　life—in your hands.
> Amen

The big view lens this prayer presents brings our smaller view into a more accurate perspective. We are reminded that we are not the center of the world, and the choices we make impact a much bigger story. Reciting the words of the Lord's Prayer helps us see that our life is shaping other lives for better or for worse every day. And the stories of Sonja Carson, Glen Holland, and a small band of Polish POWs reveal there are more lives that will be affected by us than we will ever see.

Your View of Circumstances Shapes What They Become

W hen you look at the figure below, what do you see?

It could be an old woman or a young woman, depending on the way you look at her face. From one angle, she has a big nose and a wide scarf, and her chin is pointed down.

She looks like a grandmother. But if you look at the picture from another angle, she magically morphs into a young woman looking into the distance with a feather in her hat. (As I get older, that "other angle" is of great interest to me.) The picture communicates without words a profound truth: the way you choose to look at something changes what you see.

The same thing can be said about our circumstances. When your eyes focus on different details, it changes the way your circumstances look. This principle is illustrated by a story my mom used to tell me when I was a child. Maybe you heard it too. It's about two boys who each received different gifts at Christmas: One got a box full of toys; the other, a small pile of horse manure. When the boys' parents walked in to the room, they witnessed a surprising sight. The boy with toys was whimpering because he couldn't make his toys work. The other boy was grinning from ear to ear. He looked up at his parents, and exclaimed, "With all this poop, there must be a pony somewhere!"

If you've heard this story before, more than likely you heard it as a lesson on optimism. But I maintain that it is also about something else. The fact is, behind the horse's mess, there *is* a horse. At this point, whether or not it belongs to the boy is up for grabs. Maybe the horse is in the next room. Maybe it's nowhere in sight. Maybe the parents are so impressed by the boy's attitude that they actually get him a horse. Maybe the boy is so inspired by his own excitement that he spends the next few years earning one. The point is, what the boy sees in front of him isn't the full story. And what happens next in this story is partly dependent on the way he *views* what he sees.

We see the impact of our perspective on our circumstances in Paul's letter to the Philippians, where he writes that his imprisonment, mockery, and pending death were reasons to rejoice. "What has happened to me has actually served to advance the gospel," he writes, sounding a bit deluded in his dire situation (Phil 1:12). However, time has revealed that the way Paul viewed his circumstances was, in fact, accurate. Millions of people have been influenced by the words Paul wrote during his prison sentence.

However, it's important to note that when he wrote these words, Paul did not have the hindsight we have looking back at his situation. Instead, he chose to look at his circumstances through a different lens, much like the boy in my mom's story. Paul saw solitude as an opportunity rather than a setback, because he had time to write letters to people he had not yet reached. He saw his imprisonment inspiring others to share the gospel, which increased its impact, even if some of them were not driven by motives he preferred. He faced death willingly, instead of fearfully, because he knew death would not be where God's story for him would end (Phil 1:15-21). Because of this perspective, Paul was able to write one of the most hopeful and inspiring letters of the New Testament. And the reason his letter has touched so many lives is partly due to his circumstances while writing it.

Paul's words reveal that hope doesn't just come from what happens *around* us; hope comes from the perspective we have *in* us. This is a truth we can take into every circumstance we face. You may not be able to change what is going on around you, but you can choose the way you see. And this can make a difference in how your circumstances unfold.

In 1955, Martin Luther King Jr. preached a sermon titled, "Looking Beyond Your Circumstances." It was eight years before his "I Have a Dream" speech that would change America's course. In this lesser-known sermon, Dr. King suggests that one of the great temptations is to become too absorbed in our circumstances, which leads to the conclusion that changing our circumstances is the only way out of them. Under that mindset, Dr. King states, our personality becomes "thinner and thinner, ultimately disintegrating under the pressing load." Martin Luther King concludes that *we* are part of the equation in determining the outcome our circumstances give to us. Seeing that can change everything.

GREAT BEGINNINGS

My grandfather's story was a legend we heard many times growing up, a true tale embedded in our family history. Each time I heard it, it nurtured the traits of perseverance and grit that run through my Serbian veins. With the recent struggle our country has had with whether to keep immigrants out, it's ironic to think that some of our country's best stories began with letting immigrants in.

At least my family certainly thinks so.

Todor Pero Polich left Serbia in 1906, at the time when his country was struggling under Austro-Hungarian rule. Like a multitude of immigrants across the globe, he came to America to make a new start. Boarding a boat by himself, he traveled two and a half weeks across the Atlantic, accompanied by no one he knew. At the age when I graduated high school, my grandfather left his homeland, never to return.

He knew no English when he arrived. His possessions consisted of a dollar in his pocket and the clothes on his back. After he got off the ship at Ellis Island, he traveled by train to California, where his fifth cousin gave him a job washing dishes. With only a few English words and very few contacts, he was lucky to get even that. However, Todor never limited himself to the way his circumstances might have looked. Instead, he viewed each circumstance as part of his journey and persevered to where they would lead him next.

Forty-one years later, my grandfather sold his first construction company for $7.5 million. That amount doesn't sound like much until you realize that the year was 1947. After Todor sold his company, he started a second construction company, which he turned over to my dad after he retired. The money he made in his businesses didn't only foot the bill of many of his grandchildren's college education (including mine), it also contributed toward building several Orthodox churches that still stand today.

Yet in spite of his financial and material success, my greatest memory of my grandfather consists of two words he repeated over and over until the day of his death. To this day I cannot read those words without hearing them in his deep Serbian voice. He would lean in close and repeat them to me every time he had a chance:

"Morale and character," he'd say, with a tremor in his voice. (Although with his accent it sounded like *modal* and *chadacter*)

"Thees is most important," he'd whisper, shaking his long bony finger up to my face.

"Never forget, Lauritza Annitza."

And I never did.

Morale is defined as a person's courage, optimism, and determination. *Character* consists of the distinctive qualities and reputation that sets a person apart. These two words helped my grandfather persevere in his circumstances instead of disappearing under their weight. Somehow he believed that the way he lived his circumstances, rather than the circumstances themselves, would make a bigger impact on the way things turned out. He was right.

My grandfather looked at each chapter of his life as giving him strength and fortitude, knowing it was shaping him for the dreams that were ahead. He believed each circumstance was equipping him for where he was going and paving the road to what was next. The vision he had for more than what was immediately in front of him ended up charting his course.

With the lens of the big view, we diminish the power our circumstances have over us. And we are buoyed by the truth that the way our circumstances look is not always an accurate indicator of what is ahead.

AN UNLIKELY PATH TO A PRESIDENCY

As a child, I remember vaguely hearing about a man serving a twenty-seven-year sentence for wanting what his people deserved. But my adult eyes watched as that man emerged from his prison cell and four years later was elected president of a sovereign state. Under this man's leadership, an entire nation was transformed.

For the twenty-seven years that I moved freely from childhood to adolescence, and then adolescence to adulthood, Nelson Mandela lived every day in prison, with the same schedule, the same limitations, and the debilitating structure of prison life. He spent nearly a third of his life in captivity. However, in more than one interview, Mandela said he learned things in those twenty-seven years that uniquely prepared him for his presidency. Though Mandela would not have chosen the route he was forced to take, it was clear his circumstances shaped him into the person he became.

While he was in prison, Mandela informed his ideals through books he disciplined himself to read and built bridges of friendship with enemy prison guards to widen his grace. He never surrendered to a sedentary life. When he finally emerged from prison, it took little time for his country to recognize their new leader. But the time Mandela spent in adversity helped make him the leader he turned out to be.

When we see our circumstances with the long view in mind, it empowers us to live them well, because we are viewing our circumstances as an important part of our story. Difficult circumstances shape what happens to our character and often position us for what our story will become, but we usually see this only in hindsight. Keeping this perspective in front of us enables us to persevere with promise and hope. It was apparent in my grandfather's eyes that we were the dream he saw when he faced adversity, and we were the story he wanted to finish when a chapter looked bleak. The vision of things ahead caused him to live his circumstances the way he did.

If we don't see our circumstances with the lens of the big view, we may draw conclusions, based on our limited view, that could alter what happens next. Certainly that was true for Nelson Mandela, for at any time in those twenty-seven years he could have surrendered in despair to the apparent realization that prison would be his life. History now shows that prison served as preparation for his life; however, Mandela didn't know that when he was living it. He made a decision not to give in to despair, and his grit and perseverance helped him make the next good choice in front

> When we see our circumstances with the long view in mind, it empowers us to live them well.

of him. The way he grew in grace and knowledge while in prison gave him a deep well to draw from in his presidency.

Though our story is somewhat limited by the circumstances we are given, the stories threaded through the Bible support the fact that we play a significant part in how our story gets written. The narratives indicate that God writes our story *with* us, not around us, and our story evolves by the way we respond to each scene. God's overall plan may be secure, but we have been given freedom for how we live our part.

Looking at what is happening *to* us as building something *in* us helps us view our circumstances as giving us something we need for the path ahead. This can infuse us with hope and optimism in those seasons when we are waiting for something to change. Our faith is stretched when the path is long and the route seems unclear. But during those times, God does his finest work in writing our story—if we can hold on until he is through. And if we need encouragement to press on, there are stories we can turn to when we are tempted to lose hope.

A LONG AND TWISTED PATH

If he was honest with himself, he noticed her attraction immediately. From the time he started working for her husband, there had been sly looks and admiring stares, but he thought if he paid no attention, they would eventually go away. Smelling her perfume in the hallway, he tried to ignore the fact that she was hovering nearby. But when the door closed and he looked up, his face grew white. Half naked and beautiful, she stood in front of him, beckoning him close.

I can't do this, his thoughts screamed, but the words emerged as a whisper.

Softly, she placed her hand on his shoulder and lured his neglected body into her embrace. Without a moment for a second thought, he jerked from her grip and ran; his mind a blur and his body trembling from the shock. Out of the door he flew, heaving and gasping and running until suddenly he looked down at his body and froze.

He had left what he was wearing in her hands.

When his boss came home, Joseph knew from a single look what she had done. The clothing she ripped from his chest had supported her lies, and now Joseph would pay for rejecting her.

Alone in his jail cell, he contemplated the circumstances that had brought him to this place. "Unfair!" he cried, and it was, but no one was there to listen to his side. Sentenced for a crime he did not commit, he had no idea when or if he'd ever be released.

Days passed, and eventually he girded himself up. Seeing no one but the jailer, he befriended him and resolved to survive his days. Someday his resiliency would pay off, he told himself, no matter how hopeless things looked. As he drifted off to sleep, a small voice in the back of his head reminded him that if that dream he had as a young boy were true, this jail cell would not be where he would end up.

When he awakened, two men were asleep in his cell, each awaiting the outcome of an accusation. When they woke up, it was apparent they had a fitful sleep, and as they discussed their dreams, Joseph's heart stirred. The men saw his expression and prodded him to speak, and when they were released to face their sentence, the accuracy of Joseph's interpretation was soon apparent.

Joseph was filled with optimism, believing it would be just a matter of time before one of them came back. When a year passed and no one came, his hope for release grew dim. Still he refused to give up.

When the morning came that the jailer approached his cell, two full years had passed. Joseph thought he knew every expression on the warden's face, but this was a face he'd never seen. Joseph was being summoned by the king. Numb, Joseph emerged from his cell, and the palace official repeated the story of why he had come. The king had a troubling dream, and a servant had remembered a "dream interpreter" in jail. If Joseph could interpret the king's dream, he would be raised up and rewarded in ways that would change his life.

As Joseph was led through the prison gate, fresh air caressed his face and he moved through the streets, feeling like he was in a dream. When he gave his interpretation and was raised to a position under the king himself, Joseph realized he *was* in a dream. His own (see Gen 37–41).

When we turn in our Bibles to Joseph's story, we often view his life at the speed we read. Reading the sentence, "After two full years had passed," takes three seconds, yet the thought of actually *living* those years is something altogether different. Digesting these phrases in light of his whole story can bring perspective in our own, especially when we are in the midst of circumstances that feel very dark. We see that an unfair prison sentence positioned Joseph for the palace, and God used that time to shape him into the leader he became. What happened *inside* him, because of what happened *to* him, equipped him for his leadership.

The stories of Joseph and Mandela help us see the big view of our lives, and understand that things may be viewed differently when we look back. We can see each circumstance as positioning us for what is coming, and this gives us motivation to persevere when things look dark. We can't always see what might be directly ahead. But often when we look back on the timing and detail of our circumstances, we see evidence of an unseen Conductor, who is cheering us on.

> We can see each circumstance as positioning us for what is coming, and this gives us motivation to persevere when things look dark.

A DIFFERENT LENS FOR A DARK TIME

Sitting silently in a movie theater in 1997, I stayed frozen in my seat for several moments after the film was through. The final scene had showed a small boy who had emerged from captivity in a prison camp, and he was perched on a giant tank. Flanked with American soldiers on either side, his expression was joyous. He had won the game.

In reality, the boy had not been in a game; he was held prisoner with his father in a World War II concentration camp. To keep his son protected from the horror of their surroundings, the father created an imaginary game, reframing the child's perspective so he could survive this dark time. He told him that points were only given to children who hid from prison guards and didn't complain—no matter how difficult their circumstances became. If he cried or said he was hungry, he would lose points, but if he stayed hidden and quiet, he would make points. The first child to reach a thousand points would win the game, and the prize was a giant life-sized tank.

There are scenes in the prison camp that cause the child to suspect that the game is a farce. But the father reinterprets each scene to suspend the child's belief. As the audience, you are swept into the fantasy of the child's point of view. By shaping his son's perspective, the father creates a reality that enables his son to survive the prison camp, and his ability to do that in the midst of such horror is captivating. The title of the movie, *Life Is Beautiful*, is a summary of the father's perspective. He is able to pass on to his son this view of life, even when life has become anything but.

Just before the final scene, the father is taken by a prison guard and led to his execution. Yet the audience sees through the boy's eyes that his father marches joyfully, as if he is going to receive a great prize. The father's last words to his son are instructions for the final round of the game: he must hide in a small sweatbox until he hears no more noise. When the boy finally emerges, he becomes ecstatic as he is swept up by American soldiers who place him on top of their tank.

Under the backdrop of this scene, the child—now an adult—narrates his ride to freedom while reflecting on the fact that his father's perspective had saved his life. All the way up to his execution, his father had made a choice to create a picture of life and hope in the midst of death and despair, and the boy thanks his father for giving him that gift.

Our perspective in difficulty can be more important than the difficulty itself in determining the affect it has on our lives. In *Man's Search for Meaning*, Viktor Frankl argues this premise from his experience in a prison camp, and says that in despair we are given a unique opportunity to see life in a new and fuller way. He observed that one of the surprising benefits of living in a dark place was how it gave the prisoners the ability to see beauty in a way they had never seen it before. He recounts moments when, at the end of a day, a few prisoners would look up at the sky and drink in every color and nuance of the sunset. If music was heard in the distance, they trained their ears to hear it, and if a poem or song was shared in the evening, they let it breathe life into them for another grueling day.

Frankl observed that excruciating circumstances created the opportunity to view life differently from when things were "normal." Perhaps you have noticed this yourself. Priorities shift, senses heighten, and beauty and goodness you do not usually notice suddenly rise to the surface. Like water for those who thirst, the smallest treasures we see quench our parched souls. For those reasons, we can view difficulty as a gift.

Life Is Beautiful emphasizes the power of our perspective by suggesting that a small boy could remain undamaged by the horror around him because his eyes were directed toward challenge and hope. This was the gift the child's father had given him. And perhaps we can say it's the same gift that God offers to us. Frankl observed that the prisoners who knew God carried a view of suffering which allowed them to bear their sufferings differently. They were able to see themselves not as victims of suffering but as candidates for a higher call. They saw difficulty as an opportunity to deepen their spiritual life, and wanted to be "counted worthy" of the sufferings inflicted on them. The challenge of this calling, much like the "game" for the son in the film, succeeded in fueling their vision and strength. Thus they resolved to live well in their circumstances, whether they lived or died. Their eyes were on a story that would outlive their own.

EYES TO SEE WHAT WE DON'T SEE YET

Paul emphasizes the importance of perspective in our circumstances, saying, "We fix our eyes not on what is seen, but on what is unseen, since what is seen is temporary, but what is unseen is eternal" (2 Cor 4:18). With these words, Paul indicates that we should view our circumstances as transitory, which we know by experience they actually are. We have only to see someone win the lottery and then lose it all, build a mansion and then get hit by a tornado, or begin as a dishwasher and end up owning a company to recognize that what is happening right now isn't always the way things will be. And what will be often unfolds from the way we see.

It was this belief that caused Martin Luther King Jr. not only to write a sermon about looking beyond circumstances, but to look at his own circumstances with different eyes. And America began to catch his vision from the steps of the Lincoln Memorial where he laid out his dream for all to see. Reflecting on the importance of perspective, Dr. King gives a hint of what inspired his speech on that historical day: "Whenever we look merely at our circumstances we end up with a frustration shrouded with devastating cynicism. This is why it is necessary to look beyond our circumstances for something fixed and permanent which can master every circumstance." For Dr. King, this "something fixed and permanent" was God. And believing God was greater than his circumstances allowed him to say what he believed would one day be.

Your circumstances are not the full story, they are part of the story and are working together with your response to make the story what it will become. With the lens of the big view, you are inspired to live well in each of your circumstances, because you see the power of your response to them in how your story unfolds. And how your story unfolds will be your legacy.

3

How Your Death
Changes Your Life

I originally titled this chapter, "Ten Out of Ten Die." My editor didn't think it would fly. But the truth is, ten out of ten *do* die. And if you stop and let that sink in for a minute, it can actually be the best thing to happen to your perspective. One day, you— along with everyone around you—will be gone. And there is a pretty good chance you'll get no warning when that will be. It's a fact you may try to medicate yourself from, avoid thinking about, or attempt to beat with cryogenics, but death is one in- evitability no one can escape. However, there is one thing we *can* do about our death. We can let it wake us up.

When I was in seminary, one of my first professors was Ray Anderson, a brilliant man who was almost responsible for prematurely ending my seminary career, because on the first day of class, I didn't understand a single word he said. But I hung in there and even picked up a few phrases that stayed with me. Most memorable was the phrase "agogic moment," which he used to describe what it means when a person "wakes up" and is personally addressed by something greater than him- or herself.

The phrase was originally coined by the French author Jacob Firet, and he used it to describe those moments when the volume gets turned up, the blinders are stripped away, and you are suddenly met by something bigger than yourself. Maybe you've been there:

You look up, and see a million stars.

A sunset stuns you.

A preacher speaks, and suddenly you are the only one in the audience.

A sentence in a book grabs you.

A diagnosis is handed to you.

A part of you that was asleep is now fully awake, and for a moment you think and act differently. You breathe a little deeper. Move slower. Look at people (or yourself) in a different way. Important things surface above the urgent things, and your perspective is changed, even if it's only for a moment.

Firet describes this "agogic moment" as set apart from other moments because it carries a transformative power, "a motive force" that activates the person it is focused on. This "force" is something—or maybe more appropriately Someone—who inhabits the words you hear or the event you are a part of, and addresses you at a deep level. You are "spoken to" in a way that opens you up to see things you haven't seen before, exposing truth and inspiring change.

Both Jacob Firet and Ray Anderson emphasized the fact that the agogic moment comes through an ordinary event; it is not a supernatural, Ouija-board experience. It's a moment that becomes extraordinary because of the way the person receives it. I remember Ray Anderson explaining in class that as ministers or helpers we cannot create the agogic moment for someone else; we can only make room for it. This motive force is initiated by God alone, and its affect is determined by the person who receives it.

The awareness of our mortality can give us this moment. For that reason, a death scare, or even a death consciousness, can be a gift. The opportunity to see our death in front of us can be an opportunity to see our lives in a new way. We get jolted out of our "I'm going to be here forever" stupor, and our perspective shifts. We have the urge to hug our child tighter, appreciate our spouse more, love our friends better, and care more about people in need. For a moment we are stopped in our tracks. And some deep questions rise to the surface. *What if I died tomorrow? What will I leave behind? How will I be remembered?*

Sometimes the moment takes hold and lasts for a little while. But more often than not, we quickly end up back in our routines, back to our schedules, back to the busyness that consumes our days. Until, the next moment. And the three questions come back again.

> The opportunity to see our death in front of us can be an opportunity to see our lives in a new way.

If we hover long enough in those moments, meditating on these questions can give our perspective a gift when life sucks us back in. These questions can move us from an agogic moment to authentic life change, depending on how we let their answers touch and shape our lives. For this reason, these questions will serve as a framework for the rest of this chapter's thoughts.

WHAT IF I DIED TOMORROW?

Driving up California I-5 in 1989, I was headed to a big conference in the Bay Area. I had just started working for Youth

Specialties, a prominent youth ministry organization, and they were having a youth workers' conference in which I was scheduled to speak for the very first time. As I made the long drive, my mind was filled with thoughts about my presentation. I wondered how would I do, whether people would like me, and what would happen if (God forbid) I went blank in the middle of my talk. Suddenly, my thoughts were briefly interrupted by a noise that sounded like a flat tire. When my car was able to keep driving, I wrote it off as a false alarm.

When I got to my exit on the freeway, my car immediately came to a screeching halt. Cars were stacked behind each other on a normally quiet off-ramp, and I knew something odd was going on. So I rolled down my window and motioned to the guy in the car next to me to do the same.

"What's going on? Is there a concert or something?"

He gave me a surprised (and slightly sympathetic) look. "You don't know? There's been an earthquake."

Thinking back, I vaguely remembered a few cars pulled over to the side of the freeway when I thought I had a flat tire. I just didn't pause long enough to make the connection. It turns out the earthquake measured 6.9 on the Richter scale and was the largest quake San Francisco had seen since 1906. By the time the night was through, 63 people were dead, 3,757 were injured, and thousands were left homeless. Needless to say, the conference I was headed to was canceled.

As I made my way to wait out the earthquake's aftereffects at a friend's house in Palo Alto, I was struck by how quickly my mindset changed. I wondered what condition my friends would be in when I got there, and how to let my family know I was okay. My friend's house was dark when I arrived, so we lit candles and huddled next to the radio.

The next day we drove to a house that had been pummeled by the quake to try to help a woman wade through the debris that had been her house. As it gradually became clear that people had lost their lives just miles from where I was, I found myself contemplating some big questions: *What if one of those deaths had been me? Would I be okay if life ended at this moment? Would there be anything I wished I had done differently?*

A second thought occurred to me while I was processing the disaster's effects. In an earthquake, *where you happen to be* matters. In fact, where you are standing matters more than how strong the shaking is. Two of the biggest stories to come out of the 1989 earthquake were the collapse of the Nimitz overpass and the cracking of the San Francisco Bay Bridge. The Golden Gate Bridge, which was built decades before either of the other two structures, stood firm even though it had none of the benefits of modern architecture. Because of this earthquake, people discovered that the Golden Gate Bridge had an advantage over other bridges that proved to be most important of all: its foundation.

Completed in 1937, the Golden Gate Bridge's foundation was built into bedrock, so it was able to withstand the severe shaking much better than either of its modern counterparts. This brought to the surface a very important perspective involving construction in California: the foundation that holds a structure is more important than how elaborately the structure is built. A building may be the envy of all architects in its complexity and beauty, but if it's built on the wrong foundation, especially in California, it has the capacity to fall with a great crash.

Jesus tells a story that gives us a similar lesson. Except instead of bridges, he uses houses; instead of earthquakes, he uses storms; and instead of being on a shore in California, he's on the shore of Galilee. The story is positioned at the end of of Jesus' longest-recorded speech. The topic of his speech was life management, but people refer to it as the Sermon on the Mount. Since there was a lot of buzz about Jesus at that time, many people came to hear what he had to say. And at the end of his speech, he told this parable:

> Everyone who hears these words of mine and puts them into practice is like a wise man who built his house on the rock. The rain came down, the streams rose, and the winds blew and beat against that house; yet it did not fall, because it had its foundation on the rock. But everyone who hears these words of mine and does not put them into practice is like a foolish man who built his house on sand. The rain came down, the streams rose, and the winds blew and beat against that house, and it fell with a great crash. (Mt 7:24-27)

I was taught in seminary that when a parable gives us a comparison of two things, the way to discover the point of the parable is to look at the similarities and differences between them. In this story, both men are house builders, so this isn't a parable about whether to build a house. In fact, it's fair to say that the way Jesus tells this story, he presumes everyone is a house builder. Additionally, both houses face a storm, so this isn't a parable about storm avoidance. The variable in the story is *where* the houses are built.

The point Jesus is making is similar to what the Bay Area bridges revealed in the earthquake: when a storm hits, your foundation makes the difference. Jesus' underlying message in this parable is that storms cause us to look at what is critically important about life. What we view as important might not be what is really important, and the end of our lives will reveal the truth. This parable reminds us that w*hat we build our life on* will be the only thing left standing when the storm takes us away.

The crowd is left with the possibility of an agogic moment. And when we come face to face with our death, so are we. It's an opportunity to look closely at our lives, and if necessary make a change. Mr. Holland discovered the meaning of his life when he stood in the auditorium in the final scene of the movie. In that moment he realized the accomplishments he once dreamed of having could never have matched the legacy of how he lived.

What will be left standing at the end of our lives? Jesus' parable confronts us with this question, encouraging us to consider what is lasting. When the storm takes us away, what we have built our lives on is all that will be left.

WHAT WILL I LEAVE BEHIND?

Turning fifty brings all kinds of interesting issues into a person's life, not the least of which is the question of life insurance. You are now officially on the back nine of life. Unlike a sudden diagnosis, aging is more of a vague awareness of death. You know it's coming, but instead of being at your door, it's down the street a little. At least as far as you know.

My husband has life insurance, but I have informed him he can't go first because I will lose him *and* our son (because he is not mine biologically), and it won't matter if I have money. But all these conversations about wills and insurance prompt me to think about other investments I should make before I go, and what I want to leave with people when my time comes. It also makes me think about how I don't really want to think about these things at all.

But they are good things. Reorienting things. Things that have to do with where our priorities are, and where we want them to be. And if we are still breathing, we have time to switch things up. Jesus offers some brief remarks in another part of the Sermon on the Mount that add clarity to the discussion. His words offer a perspective on what we will leave behind as we contemplate the back nine of life:

> Do not store up for yourselves treasures on earth, where moth and rust destroy, and where thieves break in and steal. But store up for yourselves treasures in heaven, where moth and rust do not destroy, and where thieves do not break in and steal. For where your treasure is, there your heart will be also. (Mt 6:19-21 NIV 1984)

Then, right after these verses, Jesus says, "The eye is the lamp of the body. If your eyes are healthy, your whole body will be full of light."

The close proximity of these two teachings seems to indicate that our treasure is connected to our perspective. Jesus seems to be saying that *where our treasure is stored* is a sign of what we view as important. One way to see what is important to you is to look at your checking account or credit card bill. The investments you've made are a good filter to determine what you value in life. But here's a potentially ominous thought if you have a lot of income, and a hopeful thought if you don't. No matter how strategic you are with your money, one day it will be left behind. Even if you designate where it should go, someone else will eventually take over your property, your bank account, and all of your financial investments. However, your investments of words and actions will leave permanent deposits that will carry on eternally after you're gone.

If you think for a minute, I bet you can remember words that lodged somewhere inside you and maybe even changed the trajectory of your life. What were some of those words? And maybe more importantly, who spoke them?

As I was nearing the end of my high school years, I was living through the tumultuous reality that my parents were headed for divorce, and I was soon headed to UCLA to major in theater arts. Somewhere in the middle of all that, I went to a Young Life camp and heard a message that God

> Your investments of words and actions will leave permanent deposits that will carry on eternally after you're gone.

loves me and wants to do life with me. It was one of my first agogic moments, even though at that point I didn't know what that was. The volume was turned up, and I invited God to have my life, but I came home to the same life I had when I left. However, there was a seed in me that held a future I couldn't have imagined.

There was one man, though, who could imagine it. He was the father of one of my closest friends. I had observed that he and God were close, and apparently he saw some spiritual potential in me and decided at a most unexpected moment to say something to me about it. His daughter and I were nursing a hangover from a concert we attended the night before, and we were trying to sneak into her kitchen to grab a piece of toast when we bumped into her dad. Expecting his disdain over our obvious condition, I was more than surprised when he decided instead to choose that particular moment to speak into my life. These were the words he said:

"Laurie, I think you will go to seminary someday."

I nearly choked. He was dear, but deluded.

Ten years later when I sat in Ray Anderson's class and thought about agogic moments, I realized that had been one for me. My friend's father was Neil Clark Warren, and at the time he was the dean of psychology at Fuller Seminary. He eventually went on to become the founder and former CEO of eHarmony.com.

I have often thought back to that moment, wishing I had said back to him, *Dr. Warren, I think someday you will begin an online dating service that will be responsible for hundreds of thousands of successful marriages.* To which he would have replied (given that the Internet hadn't been invented), "What's online?"

The point is, I never forgot his words. They took root in me somewhere, an investment in the trajectory of my life. When I think about treasures that will outlive me, investments like that come to mind. There are so many words we don't say—to our children, our spouses, our parents, our friends. Things we think but never get out of our mouths. Things we want to do with people but never have the time. Then the end stands in front of us, and suddenly the thought occurs to us, *What if I don't get the chance?*

Contemplating our death urges us to make these investments before it's too late. The good news is, we don't need money to make them. We just need to make the time. And my seminary degree is proof that one word or action can change the trajectory of someone's life.

HOW WILL I BE REMEMBERED?

Since finding myself on the back nine of life, I've noticed that time moves twice as fast, and doubles its speed with each year. I find myself holding years and nongray hairs with equal futility. Sometimes this awareness of the shortage of time comes as a dawning; other times it's a sudden flash. We see the span of our lives for the length it actually is: short, miniscule even. In light of the grand scheme of eternity, our lives are but a flicker. However, the imprint we make while we are here carries on after our life is through. It is an imprint that influences other lives and can even be responsible for how some of those lives end up.

A couple of years ago the story of a plane crash grew more horrific with the recovery of the airplane's black box. This piece of evidence revealed what had actually happened. Apparently after takeoff, the pilot left the cockpit to use the restroom. After he exited, the copilot locked the cockpit door. It was later determined that at that point the plane left its intended trajectory and nosed down toward a purposeful crash. As the plane began to plummet, the pilot could be heard shouting for his copilot to open the door. Faint screams came from the cabin just seconds before the crash. Then, silence.

> The imprint we make while we are here carries on after our life is through.

The copilot, it was later discovered, suffered from depression. Flight 9525 became his decision to end his life. Tragically, 149 people who did not make that decision went with him.

We hear many messages telling us "Your life is just about you." However, in an instant the world saw a vivid picture of just the opposite. The wreckage on the French Alps in 2015 displayed the universal truth that our stories don't belong just to us. They move through us to touch and affect other lives. Our actions don't only influence other people, they become our legacy, and the pain or joy we share with others is how we will be remembered.

Though most of us will never experience the truth Flight 9525 reveals in such a dramatic way, a tragedy like this makes us aware of the impact our stories have. The things we carry—our experiences, our sorrows, and our blessings—move through us in conscious and unconscious ways, and the decisions we make in our personal stories affect others in ways we might not be aware of or see. Keeping the big view in front of us, we become inspired to allow what's in us to touch others in a life-giving rather than life-taking way, and are inspired to leave this world better than when we came. Coming to this awareness is a journey a depressed copilot failed to take. We honor the lives he took with him by learning from the perspective we gain from this tragedy.

Then we learn to live *with* that perspective.

MAKING YOUR LIFE COUNT

In the summer of 2014 a small craze swept social media, and within a couple weeks it had reached people all over the world. Dubbed "The Ice Bucket Challenge," it was a fundraising effort by the ALS Association to raise money for and awareness about amyotrophic lateral sclerosis, commonly known as Lou Gehrig's disease. To participate, a person made a video of a bucket of ice water being dumped on their head, posted it on Facebook or Instagram, and challenged three friends to do the same. The friends had twenty-four hours to accept the challenge or donate $100 to ALS. Most people who were challenged ended up doing both.

Computer screens everywhere were filled with images and videos of people dumping water and donating to the cause. I discovered that the year before it escalated, the Ice Bucket Challenge had raised $1.7 million for ALS. But in the summer of 2014 that number catapulted to $6 million. What happened?

With a little bit of research, I discovered more about the man who propelled the Ice Bucket Challenge to its ethereal heights. Pete Frates was a college baseball player who was diagnosed with ALS in 2012. After coming to grips with the heartbreaking news, Pete decided that instead of spending his days privately grieving, his diagnosis had put him in a unique opportunity to raise awareness for the disease. He immediately dedicated himself to speaking at fundraisers and ALS events, but by July 2014, ALS had taken his voice. Thinking his window of opportunity was over, fate took a God-breathed turn when a friend introduced him to the Ice Bucket Challenge. Pete made a video of himself bobbing his head in his wheelchair to the song "Ice, Ice, Baby," which played in the background. He posted it and challenged a few friends to dump ice water on their heads. Unbeknownst to him, the craze had begun.

As the challenge lit fire and spread through the gasoline of social media, Pete Frates realized he needed to take the challenge himself. No longer able to speak or walk, he had a bucket of water dumped on his head at Fenway Park, the place he once dreamed of playing his beloved sport. The video of Pete taking the challenge spread rapidly, and by the end of August, ALS had raised nearly $6 million toward ending this debilitating disease. To date, ALS has raised $115 million because of the Ice Bucket Challenge. And the motor behind it all was Pete Frates.

In the brief time after Pete was diagnosed with ALS, he managed to get married, have a baby, and raise millions of dollars to help others with this disease. Pete may not live to reap the benefits of his fundraising, but he knows that other people will benefit from the money he raised. This knowledge propelled him to not just live his days but let his story be used to make an impact. And as an added twist of irony, it was after Pete lost his voice that he was heard loudest of all.

Heroism is not just found in stories of Nelson Mandela and Pete Frates. And it could be found in us too. We don't have to arrive at a specific age to realize we only have one shot at this life. The only information we are not given is when we are in the last scene. It could be now. It could be years from now. But how would you live the scene you are in if you knew it was your last? Keeping that question in front of you is how your death can change your life.

You don't have to change what is around you. Just don't miss all that is there.

LENS 2

THE PRESENT VIEW

Yesterday is gone. Tomorrow has not yet come. We have only today. Let us begin.

MOTHER TERESA

4

Seeing the Path in Front of You

Being a planner and having issues with control are traits that often come packaged with being a firstborn child. Since I was born ten months after my parents' honeymoon, my mom said I started running things when I was two. Because I have had these traits longer than I remember, much of my life has been spent planning for things I actually know by experience will not happen the way I plan them. Yet even with that knowledge, I still look ahead and plan, because it's the way I'm wired. The irony of this behavior is that the inability to stay focused on the present can actually impact the future I'm trying to control. I miss cues and opportunities around me because I am too focused on what's ahead.

What I've discovered through the wisdom of time is that keeping our eyes focused on what is in front of us is the only way to *see* the path ahead. Otherwise we can miss the doors before us that are trying to lead us forward. What is happening right now is not only taking us into our future, it is working to change us—and that can lead us to a future we might not otherwise have imagined. If we short-circuit this process or focus on what we *think* might be ahead, we may miss out on a future that is far greater than we could have conceived. Things are unfolding to a future that can only be seen through the present view lens.

A GIRL, A SURFBOARD, AND A
NEW CHAPTER OF LIFE

She had been told the waves were good, the beaches were exquisite, and the food was deliciously cheap. That was all the information Brooke needed to commit to the trip. The grind of her daily schedule had driven her to long hours that had dulled her imagination, and a week on the tranquil coastline of Nicaragua seemed the perfect remedy. What she wasn't prepared for was how the country would woo her during her stay.

It was curious, the pull. Maybe it was the break in her rhythm, but she found herself noticing details she normally didn't take the time to see. The blend of colors that painted the sky. Endless trees that each told a story, if you stopped to take a closer look. And behind the trees she discovered children and families nestled in an impoverished community that moved beyond her gaze and into her soul. Nicaragua had begun its slow pursuit of winning her to stay.

When an Internet search uncovered an opportunity for a real estate job, she knew a return visit was on the docket. It was the second trip that led Brooke to decide that Nicaragua would be her new home. There were many unanswered questions, no long-term plan. But her answers seemed to unfold as she lived her questions. A couple months after she settled in, a teacher from a special-needs school showed up at her door and informed Brooke that they desperately needed assistance. The flexibility in her schedule allowed her to answer that call, and over the next four years, Brooke helped Los Pipitos fund a school bus, pay teacher salaries, and stock school supplies. By simply responding to the needs in front of her, Brooke became the answer to this little school's prayer.

As she learned more about El Carizal, the community that initially led her to return, Brooke became starkly aware of their lack of resources for education. That led her to develop a non-profit to fund a program for unschooled kids. She also observed that the women in the community were completely dependent on the minimal (and often insufficient) income of their husbands. Seeing their gifts in the kitchen with the minimal supplies they had, she helped them form a co-op to sell their homemade jam. This small business eventually brought in enough income to sustain each of their family's needs.

As Brooke traveled back and forth from El Carizal, an open field began to capture her imagination. Staring at that unused space, she began to envision a music festival—and what that could do to bring funds in. With the love of music entrenched in the Nicaraguan culture, her idea met little resistance, and people came out of the woodwork to jump onboard. Brooke borrowed the name of a local fruit in that region and birthed the "Pitaya Festival" in 2009. It began with a few hundred in attendance. It grew to three thousand within five years. By the fifth year, Brooke's nonprofit took in $8,000. Because the Pitaya Festival grew to have national acclaim, people began to travel far and wide to attend this yearly event. What they didn't know was that it was thought up by a girl who originally came to Nicaragua for a week to surf. A girl who let her eyes lead her from one moment to the next and eventually became responsible for changing people's lives.

In *Let Your Life Speak*, Parker Palmer says, "Before you tell your life what you intend to do with it, listen for what it intends to do with you." A corner of the world is changed because an unsettled real estate agent did just that. With the present view lens, Brooke saw details around her that mingled with her imagination, and her life found a purpose she never could have dreamed.

Brooke's story illustrates that the present moment is pregnant with possibility for our future. But we have to be *in* it to *see* it. This is no small task, as it requires us to take our mind off the future or past, and put our focus on what is in front of us. If we can do that, we may discover a door before us that could eventually change our life. One door can lead to another door, which may lead us to a future we never would have dreamed.

Is there a door beckoning you to where it might take you?

OPEN AND CLOSED DOORS

One of the things that's unsettling about driving in California is that it is okay to hold your cell phone in front of you as a GPS, but it is not okay to talk into it. I know this because of the humble fact that I have received two cell phone tickets. The police officer didn't buy my reasoning that it seems a whole lot more dangerous to drive while *looking* at your phone than putting your ear up next to it. This danger is actually compounded by the fact that the GPS directions come as you go, which causes you to keep your eyes on the GPS to see where you are turning next. The map forms as you drive.

In some ways, I see this as a small parable of life. If we stay focused on what's in front of us, we can see our route to the future, because the future unfolds as we live. One turn leads to the next turn, and we discover our path as we go. Open doors move us ahead, and closed doors force us to turn around. But open and closed doors are both fertile ground for guidance.

Parker Palmer puts it this way: "Each time a door closes, the rest of the world opens up. All we need to do is stop pounding on the door that just closed, turn around, and welcome the largeness of life that is now open to our souls."

Palmer goes on to say that there is as much guidance in what *does not* happen in our lives as there is in what does—maybe more. As you think back over your own life, have you seen this to be true? When your eyes are focused on what is in front of you, you will discover God is giving you messages about where to turn. Sometimes that guidance is in the form of an open door: you apply for a job and get it; pursue a relationship and find it's mutual; create something and discover it is warmly received. But closed doors provide equally important guidance, because they force you to turn around and see what other doors open up. The irony is, those other doors often lead you to where you actually want to go, even if you didn't know it at the time. This awareness often happens slowly, which is why your best future unfolds by staying tuned in to the present.

If your eyes are only on the future, you become too fixated on the path you think you want rather than finding the path that wants you. When you are alive to the present moment and paying attention to what it shows you, you find that path. And somehow in the process, the path that beckons you becomes the path you really wanted after all. You just may not realize it until you look back.

> Your best future unfolds by staying tuned-in to the present.

FINDING OUR PATH

I went to UCLA to become a famous actress. You can see how well that went. I did, however, have the privilege of going to school with some people who actually *did* became famous, and one of them is Tim Robbins. I'm guessing that confession may have just aged me in your mind, or perhaps raises questions as to who Tim Robbins is. Think back, if you were alive, to *Shawshank Redemption*. Or *Bull Durham*. The second film offered a message not nearly as admirable as the first, however both can be streamed if you haven't had the pleasure of viewing them. The list of films he has been in is fairly extensive—and I notice he looks older with each successive film.

Unlike Tim Robbins, my own history in the acting industry began and ended with a college degree. I got a college internship at a casting agency, but while I worked there, the doors that opened and closed ended up positioning me for a very different future. As a new Christian, gazing at scripts for films like *Porky's* (please spare yourself from looking that one up) made me realize my way into acting seemed to be *around* my faith rather than through it. And God closed some doors, so the opportunity to become famous never came to pass.

The future God has in mind for us usually doesn't come in the form of one big decision involving one big door, but a thousand little decisions involving a lot of little doors. You just have to pay attention to the door you see. If it opens, it's your decision whether to go through it. If it closes, turn around until you see another option. And listen to trusted friends who will encourage you in life-giving ways along your path. By accepting the doors that close and seeing the ones that open up, you may end up where you never imagined yourself to be. That's how I ended up in ministry.

Had the ministry-career door been the one in front of me when I entered college, I would have turned and gone any other way. But like a GPS, God took me there one door at a time. He took me through the doors that opened, and strengthened my trust in him with those that closed. And a mysterious thing happened as I traveled from one door to the next: my heart changed as my path unfolded.

The path that God has you on is not just for what is happening *to* you but *in* you. Only when you look back will you see how you were prepared for your evolving life. When you stay tuned-in to your present circumstances, you will discover there is a purpose behind each one, and it is likely that purpose is beyond what you can currently imagine. Time will reveal how the experiences you are currently having will provide you with something you will eventually need.

A CHANGE WITHIN

"I'm not sure I want to have another child."

The words stung as I heard them, and they lodged themselves in my already wounded heart. My fiancé and I were in counseling at the time, and I had been growing in my role as a future stepmother. However, I was desperately holding on to the dream of becoming a real mother—a vision my fiancé had given me shortly after we met. We dreamed together of building a family, one that would include the kids he had as well as the ones we would have together. But at forty-two, the hope of birthing a child created an urgency to the timing of our relationship. I was thrilled when he proposed, though in hindsight it was too early; we were engaged just four months after we met.

Wisely, we slowed things down and took time to allow our real selves (along with our true desires) to emerge. I discovered that having kids was something he knew *I* wanted, but not as much what *he* wanted. And through our discussions I was led to a crossroads of whether or not I could live without having a biological child. Little did I know that my acceptance of this loss would have nothing to do with the relationship I was currently in.

For you, letting go might not involve a biological child. But most of us have to come to grips at one time or another with some kind of personal loss. What we discover through the present view lens is that God often uses our current circumstances to pry our fingers from things we *think* we cannot live without. He may not take those things out of our lives, but it is our willingness to live without them that God makes room for in our souls.

My engagement eventually broke up. When I finally married at forty-nine, my husband and I had a conversation about whether to pull out all stops to try to have a baby or accept the fact that "our" baby would be the child he brought into our marriage. Because I had already been through the grieving of not becoming a biological mother, I had these conversations more objectively rather than clinging desperately to my desire. My former engagement had given me that gift.

As it turns out, the "baby" I was given was six years old when I got him, and the perfect age for my forty-nine-year-old self. The fact that he came packaged with another mom made his arrival different from what I initially dreamed. But my engagement prepared me to accept the package that came rather than fight for the package I wanted. And in the process, God helped me to discover that biology was only one way to receive this gift.

> You are here—right where you are—for a reason. Not knowing what the reason is could be your journey of faith. For faith is lived in the midst of the unknown and unseen.

Sometimes, what is happening now opens a door that changes our future circumstances. Other times, what is happening in the present unlocks a door that changes us.

You are here—right where you are—for a reason. Not knowing what the reason is could be your journey of faith. For faith is lived in the midst of the unknown and unseen.

RESTING IN THE NOW

If you turn in your Bible to Matthew 6, you will find three words that leap off the page. (This may have to do with the fact that in my Bible, the words are set apart in a different font.) The words are, *Do not worry.*

It's the one piece of advice none of us keep. Especially when our eyes are off the present and are focused on what *might* be ahead. It is helpful to note that throughout the Bible, and specifically in Exodus 3, God calls himself "I AM," which gives us a clue that God dwells *in the present*. In the context of the Exodus passage, Moses asks God who he should tell the people sent him, and God's response almost feels as if it is written in the wrong tense: "Tell them I AM sent you." Moses discovers in the rest of the passage that this "wrong tense" is actually where God lives. God is always in the present; when we are dwelling in the future or the past, we are there without him.

When Moses wants assurance for what will happen when he confronts Pharaoh, God essentially tells Moses that he can't give him that assurance until Moses is there (Ex 3:12). God does not call himself "I WAS" or "I WILL BE," although we know by experience that he is all those things. But remembering God as "I AM" is a helpful insight when we are concerned about a future that doesn't exist until we are there.

We have a God who dwells in the present. Because God exists outside time, we always experience him in the now. So when we are focusing on the future or the past, we are removing ourselves mentally from where God is. With this in mind, Jesus tells us in

Matthew 6 not to dwell on what's ahead. When he says, "Do not worry about tomorrow, for tomorrow will worry about itself" (Mt 6:34), Jesus is encouraging us to use the present view lens. And in the first few verses of this passage, Jesus shares why worrying is futile. He frames his thoughts with this compelling question: "Can any one of you by worrying can add a single hour to your life?" (Mt 6:27).

Oh sure, Jesus, point out the obvious. Worrying may not be adding any hours to my life, but think of how many hours it has taken away. Wait a minute . . . let me try that again. Think of how much control I am exerting on something I have no control over.

Clearly, Jesus has something here. And thankfully he embeds his question in an invitation to see how we can strengthen our trust in God for what's ahead. In the verses that follow, he points out the evidence all around us of God's care, and he encourages us to look at what is in front of us rather than focusing on something we cannot see. If I were to paraphrase his words in Matthew 6:25-34, they might read,

Look at the birds, and contemplate how God cares for them (v. 26).

See how the flowers are dressed, and marvel at their wardrobe (vv. 28-29).

Learn from the sustaining force of nature how God holds you in the palm of his hand (v. 30).

Focus on what you can do, *not what you can't do*, and life will unfold exactly as it should (v. 33).

Stay in the present with the great I AM and don't worry (v. 34).

Be happy (v. 34, Bobby McFerrin).

Perhaps the song "Don't Worry, Be Happy" was wiser than we thought. However, living it is our lifelong challenge. If we redirect our eyes to the here and now, we can feel a sense of peace and expectation, because we become aware that *here* and *now* is where I AM is. God unfolds his provision as we live, and provides strength at the moment we need it. It has been my experience that he rarely seems to do that in advance. However, the longer we walk with God, we see increasing evidence of his presence. And there are rare times when his presence is revealed in a way that we never could have guessed.

THE MISSIONARY AND THE NAIL

In 1937, Hubert Mitchell was captured by God's love and moved to make a drastic life change. With his wife and small child, he felt called to be a missionary in Indonesia and eventually was compelled to reach a small Kubu tribe in the Sumatra region. After settling his family close to where this tribe lived, Mitchell traveled on foot with a small band of people, making his way to the Djambi Mountains. The heat was stifling, but only one question preyed on Mitchell's mind: *How will I be able to explain the reality of God's love to a people whose language I hardly know?* He had been captured by the gospel message, but would they?

Soon after they had entered a jungle village and encountered the tribe, the chief stood silently in front of him, surrounded by warriors with spears and knives. With stern eyes, the chief studied the men who dared to violate the privacy of his jungle home. The tension eased somewhat as the chief was drawn in by the warm smile on Hubert Mitchell's face. The missionary sensed their interest in why he'd come, so instead of following the usual practice of presenting them with beads, buttons, and fish hooks, he embarked right away on the reason for his visit.

The group listened intently as he told them the story of how God sent his Son to suffer for the sins of all people. As he tried to explain the cross and the part it played in the death of God's Son, the chief looked as though he wanted to speak. The missionary paused and waited.

"What is Cross?" the chief asked in his native tongue.

Mitchell turned to his native worker, and he told him to cut down two small trees and strip them of their branches. They fastened two of the larger pieces together with grass, in the shape of a cross, and placed the object before the chief. The native looked at the cross and wanted to know more.

"How was Christ fastened to cross?" was his next question.

Mitchell stretched himself upon the wooden cross. Lying there with hands outstretched, he told of Jesus being nailed to the cross. A look of bewilderment came across the chief's face.

"Apa Pakoe?" (What is nail?)

"A nail is . . ." Mitchell stopped. How could he describe a nail to a tribesman who had never seen one?

Mitchell searched his gear. Nothing resembled a nail. Finally, he gave up and admitted to the chief that he could not describe what he was talking about. The chief had no further questions.

Mitchell was hungry and feeling somewhat dejected, so he reached in his bag for something to eat. He was disappointed that a moment with so much promise ended the way it did. While he was eating, God reminded him of a verse in Joshua 1:9: "Be strong and courageous. Do not be afraid; do not be discouraged, for the LORD your God will be with you wherever you go."

With these words, Hubert Mitchell was filled with faith as he ate his meal. Usually he finished his meal with some fresh jungle fruit or a piece of sugar cane, but he idly picked up a can of mandarin oranges from his supplies. He had bought two cans at a store in a jungle village while buying provisions for his trip. As he opened the can and poured the oranges into a dish, he heard a rattling sound.

In the bottom of the can we something shiny and metallic.

Picking it up, Mitchell got on his knees, thanked God, and then rushed to find the chief. The chief looked up and saw Mitchell in front of him with a look of surprise and wonderment. Mitchell extended his hand and showed him what was in it, and the chief took the nail and pressed it into his flesh. He nodded to Mitchell that he understood what he was trying to tell him about the way Jesus died.

Overwhelmed by the way Mitchell had found the nail, the chief was filled with faith and knelt with Mitchell on the floor of a grass hut to receive God's love. When the people in the village heard the story of the nail, many kneeled to open their hearts to God's love too. The chief was so overcome with the story of God sending his Son to die on our behalf that he offered to assist Mitchell and serve as a translator so Mitchell could share the good news with all of the country's tribes.

It was a missionary journey unlike any Hubert Mitchell could have imagined. But it only unfolded the way it did because God surprised him right when he needed God to show up. Mitchell had to keep his eyes focused on the present to see how God would take him from one moment to the next, and in so doing he discovered things about God he otherwise never would have known. And a can of mandarin oranges revealed just how creative God can be.

The present holds treasures that can change our lives if we stay *in* the present long enough to see them. With the present view lens, we are able to stay focused on where we *are* rather than where we were or maybe one day will be. And in our journey from one moment to the next, we discover the great I AM is with us.

Seeing the People
on Your Path

When you walk down the street, there's a good chance you see people. They may be finely or casually dressed, on their way to an event or doing an errand, standing in front of you or passing you by. You may notice their beauty or their blemishes, their lovely dress or unpleasant smell, their fancy cars or homeless signs, but you probably don't dwell on them beyond a fleeting thought.

When you get home, you probably see more people. If they live with you, you may notice different things. You may observe their expressions or habits, the music they listen to, or the food they like, how often they smile, or what makes them recoil, but what you may *not* see is who they really are. And possibly, their behavior around you reveals who you are.

What if you stopped this minute and started to *see* the people in front of you? Stopping to really look at people can take a chunk of time out of your life. But what if you lived each day with the knowledge that the people in front of you will be most of what mattered about your life? The man who invented the computer I am using seemed to realize this truth at the end of his life. Often characterized as rude, dismissive, and hostile to those who worked for him, Steve Jobs was known to fire people without notice to keep his driven work ethic alive. However, in his sister's eulogy, Jobs is described as understanding the importance of the people around him as he approached the end of his life.

Knowing his death from cancer was imminent, he spoke to his family and friends with a warmth and nostalgia not previously evident in his behavior. It appears as he came to the end, Steve Jobs realized the people around him were what mattered most.

If you realized this truth right now, perhaps you'd live the rest of this day differently. However, you might forget to notice the people around you when the busyness of life sucks you back in. Unless you were lucky enough to get a jolt to remind you to stay on task.

THE WORKOUT THAT WORKED ME

It was 6 a.m. at a gym I had found in a town that wasn't mine. I was half asleep when I climbed onto the elliptical to get my morning jolt. However, on this particular morning, that jolt came a little differently than I expected.

"Hi, brother!" the man next to me bellowed out at a volume that nearly pitched me off my machine. He wasn't addressing me but another man thirty feet away. A smile grew on that man's face as he waved back and then began his morning routine.

"I didn't know *you* were here!" he yelled to someone else across the room, and that man came over to shake his hand.

One person after another slowly ambled in as the gym greeter called out various salutations from his elliptical two machines away. "How's that grandbaby?" he asked a woman who looked to be about seventy-five. She came over to his machine to show him pictures. "I see that heart working," he shouted to a man discouraged about his last ten pounds.

Some came over and visited with him. Others walked by and waved. With each conversation he had, I learned something about the people around me that I would have otherwise barely noticed. The whole atmosphere of the gym changed as this man elicited warmth and care that spread like a blanket over the room. And each time he was asked how he was, his reply was always the same.

"God is good," he'd say with a smile. "And because of that, I'm doing good too."

That particular morning, I had to agree with him. I had randomly chosen an elliptical machine next to his. And I watched people come alive around me when they saw he was there.

In *Soul Keeping*, John Ortberg says if we are aware that God is looking at someone the same moment we are looking at them, it will change the way we respond to them. The people in front of you are no longer "fellow exercisers," "grocery shoppers," or "wait staff"; they are people with bigger lives than the roles they are in. Knowing you are only witnessing a small part of their story not only changes the way you view them, it can shape the interaction you have. And that interaction, big or small, can trigger what happens in their life next.

WHAT SEEING CAN DO

Overshadowed by the crowd, Zacchaeus knew he would have to prop himself up in order to see him. He was a head shorter than nearly everyone in his sight. But on this particular day, Zacchaeus's motivation was greater than this hurdle. From the perch of a nearby tree, he was able to watch the great teacher make his way through the crowd, and as Jesus moved closer,

Zacchaeus saw the softness in Jesus' eyes. But Zacchaeus's gaze turned to terror when Jesus stopped in front of him, betraying his carefully chosen hiding place for all to see.

"Zacchaeus, come down immediately. I must stay at your house today."

The words rang through Zacchaeus's body like a shock, and at the same time, these words sent waves of disbelief through the crowd. He had no response but to do what he was told.

As he came down the tree, the smallness of his body became apparent the minute he stood in front of his self-invited guest. Together they walked, while the disdain Zacchaeus held for being a tax collector now blanketed the One who accompanied him. It was clear from the crowd's murmurings that Zacchaeus's job had grown to define his life. He was more than that, but his choice to become a tax collector had forced him to settle into an identity that didn't include the inner workings of his soul.

Walking alongside him, Jesus' reputation plummeted. However, Zacchaeus's own reputation soon took an upward turn. After they got to his house, the declaration Zacchaeus made revealed what Jesus' treatment of him had unlocked: "Look, Lord! Here and now I give half my possessions to the poor, and if I have cheated anybody out of anything, I will pay back four times the amount."

The promise he made came on the heels of the way Jesus had treated him. As the crowd cheered, it was clear Jesus had triggered a ripple *through* Zacchaeus that shaped what happened next. This short story in Luke 19 reveals that the way we treat people may unlock something inside them that can influence what next happens in their life.

Certainly Ashley Smith discovered this to be true in 2003, when a man named Brian Nichols barged into her house and bound her up at gunpoint. Instead of cowering in her terror, somehow she had the presence of mind to read to him from *The Purpose Driven Life*. She slowly convinced him that it was not too late to turn his life around—and that even in prison God could use him to make a difference in someone's life. She also told him that future lives might be saved if he turned himself in.

Miraculously, after several hours Brian Nichols let Ashley Smith go. He surrendered to the officers surrounding the building and allowed himself to be peacefully handcuffed and sent to jail. It's impossible to know how many lives were saved by Ashley Smith's courageous act. But it's clear that by treating him as more than a criminal, she altered his intended trajectory. Because of this encounter, Brian Nichols's identity as a criminal was broken through and changed.

We don't have to experience an encounter this dramatic to recognize the power we have to affect people. On rare occasions our impact may be acute and immediate. In most cases it will be a small seed that grows when the person is out of our sight. By choosing to be fully present to the people on our path, we are prepared for the important encounters that may be brought into our life. And God only knows who might be affected by that choice.

With this awareness, we become more intentional with how we view people. We may discover that some are in our lives for what we have for them. Others come into our lives for what they have for us. And at any given moment, we may meet someone who causes us to walk away changed.

BEAUTY REDEFINED

I was taken aback the instant that I saw her. I had to look closely to be sure what I saw was right. Half of her face was completely normal, but the other side looked like the weight of gravity had dropped her features three inches down her face. Her right eye was permanently open and nonfunctioning—it was situated to the right of her nose. The right side of her mouth appeared to be paralyzed, and I imagined her limited movement would impair her voice. When she did speak, her clarity and warmth proved me wrong.

My immediate response was sympathy. But I also had a sense of bewilderment how this day was going to work out. She was the Compassion volunteer who showed up to work the table, and I had been paired with her to speak on Compassion's behalf. We were partners in our task to inspire people to sponsor a child. With my limited view, I imagined that her presence would be unsettling. I thought she might intimidate people from approaching the table to sponsor a child. However, my short sightedness was soon revealed as I began to actually *see* the woman behind the face.

As I began conversing with her, it became apparent that she looked in a different mirror from the one I used. She was engaging and self-assured, and couldn't wait to share that she and her friend sponsored *ten* kids. She was ecstatic that sharing her story with others would be an opportunity to get more of them helped.

I gazed at her face, which was slowly growing more beautiful. The more I listened to her, the lovelier she became.

As she talked about the ten kids she sponsored, she mentioned that three of them had special needs. I was inwardly startled at the irony. One of them needed $15,000 for an operation to have her tracheotomy removed; the child was now breathing normally, so it was imperative for her to get the tracheostomy tube out. Her parents couldn't afford the operation, so my new friend was raising money to help them.

In my muddled shame and wonderment, I realized God had shown up at the Compassion table. My eyes were finally opened to see the woman he had brought. The money she was raising for her Compassion child's surgery was the same amount that could have paid for her own plastic surgery.

I was stunned by her priorities and shamed by the beauty of her heart, which I could now see. The wonderment I felt walking in was exchanged with a new kind of wonder by the time I left. I had gone to the event hoping God would use me to touch people. What I didn't expect was that I would be the one touched. When we are present to the people in front of us, at any given moment God can use one of them to move us closer to the place he wants us to be. Keeping the present view lens in front of our eyes opens up that chance.

> When we are present to the people in front of us, at any given moment God can use one of them to move us closer to the place he wants us to be.

Could it be that a person is in front of you so you can have a window into the weight they carry? Or perhaps you'll notice your response to them and what that might reveal about you. But what if you lived with the perspective that someone you will see this day needs something you can give them—or that someone you will see has something God wants to give to you? Would you look closer? Walk slower? Maybe even stop? These thoughts occasionally cross my mind when I view people as obstacles to get through or competition for a place in line. I comfort myself by thinking, *Who in the world has the time to stop and see people when there are so many demands in the day*? Ironically, Someone who had more demands than me. And when I look closely at his encounters with people, I'm encouraged to live mine differently.

WHAT BEING SEEN CAN UNLOCK

She came to the well at a time when she knew she would have her space. The heat kept others away, and making the daily trek at this time would ensure her privacy. Unlike most women who looked forward to the end of the day to fulfill this task, she avoided the hour when people would gather, catch up, and relax. Coming at the time she did made her hiding apparent to anyone who took note.

As she approached the well and observed Jesus sitting there, she lowered her eyes. Thinking he would ignore her, she was thrown off guard when she heard him speak. But nothing could have prepared her for the words he spoke after she handed him the water he had asked her to retrieve. "If you knew the gift of God and who it is that asks you for a drink, you would have asked him and he would have given you living water."

She stifled a chuckle, as she now became curious about the stranger's state of mind. But as he went on to describe this water, she was outright sold at not having to make this trek again. Whatever this "living water" was, it had to be more convenient than the effort she had to make coming here day after day.

"Please, sir, give me this water," she blurted out, surprising even herself. He smiled, and softly looked into her eyes.

"Go, call your husband and come back."

The words pierced her heart, causing her to throw out her well-practiced answer to keep the conversation short. Just enough truth, so the probing would end.

"I have no husband."

For a moment he seemed satisfied with her answer. But her soul was laid bare when he opened his mouth to say what came out next: "The fact is, you have had five husbands, and the man you have now is not your husband."

The food in her stomach rose, and she suddenly felt like she might pass out. Who was he? Looking intently at his face, she stood at a crossroads of a decision that would alter her life. Staying and listening would bring her to the threshold of looking where her path had led her—it was hidden truth she worked very hard not to see. Now it lay in front of her, spoken and unearthed.

Attempting to change the subject, she was brought back by Jesus to face it. And she was surprised to discover its stronghold was diminished in the moment it was faced. What terrified her most held the key to her door of peace. By allowing herself to be seen, she would finally be set free.

After a little more dialogue, she uncovered the identity of the Jewish man she was speaking to. And walking home, she carried a lightness in her step that picked up her pace. The urgency that had drawn her to hide moved into a greater urgency to share the truth that this man had unlocked.

Her story moved others to find out what had moved her. The vulnerability she displayed in telling it caused others to come to Jesus and see for themselves (Jn 4:39-41). The woman who had structured her days to avoid being seen was the one God used to be seen by all. And because of her testimony, others became inspired to have their own lives changed.

This is such a well-known passage that I am always tempted to skim it. But mining its truth gives us great insight into how being seen can change our lives. Perhaps it is the people closest to us that we should focus on most.

MOVING OUR EYES INTO OUR HOME

Up to now I've been focused on the people "out there." But I would be remiss if I did not move to the people "in here." These are the people in our homes and our families, our neighborhoods and jobs. They are also the ones we see most frequently, for we do life with them every day. But do we really *see* them?

You may think that because you are *with* them, you can't help but see them. But I watched a marriage fall apart in my childhood home because one of the people in it didn't feel "seen."

What does it take to really *see* the people closest to us? Sometimes, it's simply noticing things that reveal who they are. Their passions and fears, expressions and behaviors; paying attention to what they are showing you is how you see. When my stepson wants to talk to me about his "ollies," I am not interested in the details of skateboarding currently dominating his conversation. But if I think about how much I love him, it changes the way I listen to him when he speaks. Suddenly, I am grateful he is sharing something important to his twelve-year-old heart. My attention to him is an opportunity to let him know that he is seen.

But what happens when there is a behavior going on with someone you love that you are trying *not* to see? Maybe an addiction is quietly disrupting your family's well being, or someone is acting in an abusive way that has put a wedge inside your heart. "Not seeing" may be required to maintain a peaceful relationship, and speaking up may upset the way your relationship has survived. But seeing people the way God wants us to brings the filter of truth, and this could change the dynamics of your relationship. You might be led to confrontation or distance, depending on the receptivity of the person involved.

Seeing people with God's eyes also brings the filter of grace. Observing the encounter Jesus had with Zacchaeus gives us the vision to see beneath people's behavior and consider why they might be acting the way they are. The four simple words "Hurt people hurt people" give us a broader perspective that invites us to view peoples' behavior with more grace, and looking at where that behavior comes from is a perspective we will explore in the next section of this book. Suffice to say, for the purpose of the present view lens, the filters of truth and grace may lead you to change some of the ways you have functioned in relationships.

But in our closest relationships, *seeing* doesn't stop with looking more closely at others; it includes the courage to let others look more closely at you. The thought of risking your vulnerability to be seen for who you are may give rise to terror within you, because once you are seen, you cannot take it back. You cannot return to the "false self" you may have constructed to

> Seeing people with God's eyes brings the filter of grace.

survive. But author and researcher Brené Brown inspires us to take that risk, claiming there is great strength in this stance. In her words, "Vulnerability is having the courage to show up and be seen when we have no control over the outcome. Vulnerability is not weakness; it's our greatest measure of courage."

The truth is, once we've experienced the freedom of "being seen" by others, we don't want to go back to a false or hidden self. We discover a newfound power in our transparency, and we want others to see us for who we really are. As John 4 illustrates, being seen can turn into our ministry.

Don't miss that opportunity.

It is recorded by Steve Jobs's sister that in the final scene of his life, Jobs fixed his gaze upon the people closest to him, and ended his life with these words: "Oh wow, Oh wow, Oh wow."

I, along with the rest of the world, wonder what he saw.

Perhaps we should look at the people in front of us *before* it's too late and say the same thing. That would give us the awe we need here and now to keep them in our sight.

LENS 3

THE REAR VIEW

Life can only be understood backwards.
But it must be lived forwards.

SØREN KIERKEGAARD

Looking at Your Past Brings Clarity

Tell me about your relationship with your father," he said, leaning back in his chair.

"Why?" I replied. "I came here to talk about something else."

My defensiveness caught me off-guard, so I watched him for my next cue. I had only been with this therapist for a short time, but I observed that he was like E. F. Hutton in those old commercials—he rarely spoke, but when he did you learned to listen. Especially to the apparently random questions he occasionally asked.

My dad was a strapping man; he was twenty-two when he had me, and I believed he hung the moon. His charisma lit up any room he entered; he made people laugh, and I loved how I felt when I was with him. When I was young he would stretch out his hand, point to everything around us, and say, "See all this? It's yours," and I knew it would be if he thought I wanted it. I was his girl, and even though he didn't know what to do with a daughter when I was born, my grandmother told him he would learn. And he did.

My mom was a beauty, and I used to sit on her dressing-room counter and watch as she put in her eyelashes one by one. Beauty was complicated in the 1960s; hair and eyelashes alone could take the whole afternoon. But I never got bored watching her. She was a princess, and my dad was a prince, and we lived in a castle, my two brothers and me. And then, life happened.

Four years after my parents divorced, my dad married a beautiful woman three years older than me, had more children, and learned with as much success as he could how to stretch his heart. But a piece of my heart got torn and never grew back the same. My mom went back to school and became a therapist, and learned a lot about herself and us. She stayed single for a while, then married a retired minister eleven years older who had four adult children. Holidays became complicated, but we learned to celebrate where we could—in fragments and family parties—and I grieve a little each time. But I also carry a great deal of thankfulness because there are lots of good things in the mix. There is love enough for all, but that love has been shaped by pain and loss and issues we carry. And apparently, I was about to learn, those issues can resurface if they are not looked at and healed.

"I'd really like to get back to what I came here to talk about," I said softly.

The tremor in my voice was apparent, but E. F. Hutton stayed silent as I tried to get back to the issue of why my breakups were so sad for me. Too sad, like a piece of me was missing or something. Something seemed a little off. He paused and waited.

We meandered back to the divorce of my parents, my dad's new wife and the small age difference between us, and his growing new family. Suddenly, it became clear that *these things* were connected to *those things*. I was surprised at the weight of the connection. I thought I had settled the past and moved on. Turns out a piece of it lodged into my gut and went with me.

Because my mom was a therapist by now, she talked about the importance of looking back in order to see your way ahead. She made it clear that we don't look back to stay back; we look back so we can choose what to take into our future. Otherwise stuff follows us without our vote. Apparently, my E. F. Hutton therapist uncovered some of that stuff, and as he gently led me through past events in subsequent sessions, I could see how some of my present behavior was tied to things I hadn't processed from my past. Emotions would crop up and reveal to me that in order to see my way forward, I had to take a look at my past.

At this point, I want to add a disclaimer to this chapter to let you know that my observations concerning the rear view are mostly based on insights I've picked up from being a teacher, pastor, and most of all, a learner. However, I am such a believer in the impact the past has on our lives that I cannot write a book about reframing our perspective without considering the clarity that comes from the rear view lens. The alternative to seeing how the past has affected us is staying stuck, blaming others, recreating past emotional roads, and wondering why certain situations cause us to feel or act the way we do. If you have ever been curious about the *whys* of your behavior, more than likely it's worth a look. You can't change what has happened in the past. But you can lessen its impact on your behavior by taking the time to look back.

The rear view can give you some answers. It can also sharpen your present view. When you are willing to look at your past, you will gain some important insights about the emotional roads you've continued to travel. Bringing those insights into your present can help you find a new route.

LOOKING BACK FOR OUR FUTURE

Looking back involves the filter of memory, which is shaped by our brain. In my brief study of how this works, I ran across a concept called "Hebb's Axiom" in a book by Curt Thompson called *Anatomy of the Soul*. I found it helpful for understanding how our memory affects our perspective. The theory essentially states that "neurons that fire together wire together." In other words, the neurons in our brain that repeatedly activate in a particular pattern are statistically more likely to fire in that same pattern the more they're activated the same way.

For those (like myself) who get lost in language like this, Thompson explains this phenomenon by suggesting the analogy that if those neurons are hikers making their way up a mountain, it is likely those hikers will use the trail already forged rather than veer off course. So if the neurons in our brain fire in a certain pattern, they will likely repeat that pattern unless they are directed purposefully another way. With this understanding of our brain activity, we can understand how we pick up things in our past that we repeat subconsciously in our future. This can be good or bad depending on what we are picking up. Thompson says that we have the power to "forge new paths" when we go back and figure out how our past has affected us, and then lose those patterns that we don't want to keep. But this process requires some knowledge of how those patterns were acquired.

The rear view holds some of those answers. By looking at grandparents and parents, siblings and birth orders, inherited traits and passed on addictions, we gain a much broader and detailed view of who we are. Looking back helps us choose the

> Looking back helps us choose the things we *want* to take into our future.

things we *want* to take into our future rather than finding things hidden in our carry-on bags. The goal is to lighten our load. We can do that by taking a look at what our gene pool packed.

A DIVE INTO THE GENE POOL

My mother was a middle child, soft spoken and mostly compliant, and when she met my dad, he was the personality she wanted to be. They got married in their early twenties, and their marriage got off to an unfortunate start because my mom's father's drinking kept him from coming to the wedding and was partly responsible for his sudden death. He died the night before my parents shared their vows. My grandmother, who was divorced from my grandfather, told my dad to wait until the day after their wedding to tell my mom that he had died—which, frankly, was a lot for a twenty-two year old to handle. He did his best, but on her first morning as a new bride, my mother moved quickly from wedded bliss to shock and awe. They postponed their honeymoon and took a quick trip to Vegas. Vegas became the cure for many things.

My dad was born with 100 percent Serbian blood, which explains the distinguished nose and dark skin. His parents were larger than life, and I remember everyone treating my grandparents as if they were celebrities. They were generous and kind, and each spoke with a thick Serbian accent. When I came into the world, I was their first grandchild, and they quickly proclaimed that I was the greatest baby ever born. When my cousin Ted arrived, he also became the greatest baby ever born. Soon after, my brother Tom came, then three more cousins and my baby brother Chip, and we were all "the greatest babies ever born." We were great because our name was Polich, and my Baba and Djedo passed on a great Serbian pride, which seeped out on all of us. They impressed upon us that family was our heritage, and we should stick together no matter what. We have tried our best to honor that code, even in the complexity of what family has become.

My mom's mom held her own as a single grandparent, and her children and grandchildren and great-grandchildren became her life. My eldest cousin dubbed her Mimi, and she was fiercely loved until she died. Mimi was the one who showed me that women could live alone if they had to, and this became courage I needed since I spent forty-nine years on my own.

Looking back at each of my grandparents, I can see how the gifts and liabilities they passed on to my parents played a part in how my parents shaped me. Seeing how my parents were shaped gives me a broader understanding of the context I was shaped in. It also brings grace to the table. Perhaps looking back at your own genealogy will do that for you too.

The book of Genesis reveals the impact of genealogy as we follow the traits and characteristics carried through Israel's line. Beginning with Abraham and Isaac's repeated act of cowardice in their marriages (Gen 20:2; 26:7), you can also note the similarity between Sarah and Rebecca in the way they push for control. When Rebecca has her dream about her twins, she can't resist the opportunity to "help God" accomplish it when she disguises Jacob for the blessing (Gen 27), much like her mother-in-law Sarah attempted to "help God" when she recruited Hagar to further Abraham's seed (Gen 16). Both women could not wait for God to make his will come to pass.

Jacob picks up this controlling nature in the way he initially lives out his calling, but his wrestling match in Genesis 32 seems to subdue this trait in later years. In Jacob's son Joseph we see how the chain of control is finally broken, as Joseph waits many long years for God to fulfill his dreams (Gen 37).

After Joseph allows himself to be shaped by his suffering, the doors of power finally open to him, and he is finally reunited with his brothers. Because of his changed appearance, his brothers don't recognize him; in subsequent encounters, we witness Joseph's process of forgiving his brothers in the many tears he sheds. Ultimately he makes room for the grace he is able to extend. In Genesis 50, when Joseph says, "You intended to harm me, but God intended it for good," it's clear he has worked through his pain and has seen the bigger picture of how God used it in his life. I believe Joseph's journey is what God desires for us all.

BRINGING IT ALL INTO VIEW

When we connect our past with our present, we unlock the mystery of why our emotions and relationships look the way they do. If we do not incorporate the understanding that comes with the rear view lens, we will probably not veer from past paths that have been forged. The goal of looking back is to embrace the healthy patterns we have received, and forge new paths where we are tempted toward familiar but dysfunctional paths we no longer want to go.

Some of our behavior comes from influence, not just genetics, but the two combine together to shape the person we become. The knowledge that nurture and nature work together in our growth can be encouraging, for it means that we can change patterns through the influence of the company we keep. Thus, the people we choose to influence us are important and strategic in our path toward growth.

> The people we choose to influence us are important and strategic in our path toward growth.

When I hit my early thirties, I personally discovered the benefit of "borrowing" moms and dads to fill the gaps that were left by my parents. The Gospels support the idea of family coming from your faith community. In Mark 3:32-35, Jesus redefines his own family as those who share his faith and life. When he is told that his mother and brothers are looking for him, Jesus replies, "Who are my mother and my brothers?" Then he looks at those seated around him and says, "Here are my mother and my brothers! Whoever does God's will is my brother and sister and mother." Jesus' words give us permission to extend our families to include those around us who support, pray for, and counsel us in ways our own families may fall short.

My father's new and growing family, combined with the fact that my faith was going in a different direction from the path my parents set forth, created space for other men and women to speak into my life. Some were teachers at Fuller Seminary, others were pastors in churches where I worked, but one man in particular became a cheerleader in my life when I needed one most. He had enough of my dad's charisma to win a place in my heart, and his zest for life and love for Jesus helped shape my spiritual path. I am eternally grateful for the gift of self-esteem he gave to me as a thirty-five-year-old single woman.

There were moms I solicited to come alongside me too, and by allowing their care and affection, I was nurtured in places my biological parents weren't able to reach. Now, as I look at our son, I am aware of how he needs other voices to contribute to his growth. My husband and I will never fill all the needs of his heart, and we are aware that he will need the extended family of a faith community to help steer his course.

It is also empowering to realize through the nurture principle that we can *choose* influences and relationships that will minimize, or heighten, certain genetic traits. The choices we make will not only affect the lives of those around us—they will impact the lives that follow us. Where there has been dysfunction in our past, we can choose relationships that will push us to change.

With new and better choices, combined with the support of others, *you* can be the one to break the chain. But you may need to rely on the help of Someone greater than yourself in order to do it.

WHAT FAITH CAN DO

Looking back on your faith trajectory, you can see whether God was called on by the people in the generations before you and whether you were taught to call on God in the home where you were raised. This may encourage or inhibit you from calling on God in your current life. Nestled within the book of 2 Timothy is a verse which reveals the influence and power of generational faith. Paul commends Timothy for his sincere faith, and he describes Timothy's faith trajectory by saying that it "first lived in your grandmother Lois and in your mother Eunice and, I am persuaded, now lives in you also" (2 Tim 1:5). With this observation, Paul reveals how Timothy was positively influenced by the presence of an active faith.

It's my observation that some of the issues causing faith struggles come from parents who either rejected faith or forced faith onto their children. Both can be detrimental in a sincere journey toward discovering one's own beliefs. Clearly Timothy had an upbringing that put him on a path toward developing a strong Christian faith, but at some point he had to choose it for himself. Paul's brief reference indicates that Timothy's grandmother and mother modeled faith that made it a path worth choosing.

Observing how faith was passed on to you can provide insight into your own faith journey, it can enlighten you as you move ahead—especially as you pass your faith onto your children. My father's background in Serbian Orthodoxy, along with my mom's journey in recovery, showed me the importance of faith—not only in life, but in health. Perhaps with that same filter I propose that the greatest help we can receive in breaking the chain from our unhealthy past is the help we get from God. This help is available to us all, and God is always ready to strengthen and guide us in this task (Jer 33:3; Ps 145:18).

A NEW PATH

By having the courage to look back, we discover what is buried deep within us that can rear its head in surprising and unexpected ways. Knowing where it comes from can limit its power; things become smaller when we understand their source. As we look ahead, we realize we cannot change what happened to us, but we can move forward in new ways. Clearing new trails requires work, but with God's help, we can move off the paths we no longer want to travel and choose a healthier path.

> Clearing new trails requires work, but with God's help we can move off the paths we no longer want to travel and choose a healthier path.

Doris and John were married for seven years, and in their brief marriage they had two boys. When they divorced, the two boys stayed with Doris, and John moved up the street. Doris drank too much, so after a couple of years, the boys moved in with John. Doris died a few years later, and the boys grew up with a chasm in their hearts.

When they became adults, the older boy stayed in New Jersey, and the younger boy moved to California. The younger son was handsome and dated many girls, but because of his past with a distant mother, he was drawn to the girls who didn't like him back. He found a strange familiarity in the pattern of trying to win their love. Eventually he married the one who liked him least of all.

After she left him, the younger brother decided to look back at the well-worn paths of his past and set his sights on a new course. He began dating a woman who slowly responded with mutual affection, and though it was unfamiliar to him, he took a different path with her. She had been through her own quest of understanding her past with an E. F. Hutton therapist and was ready for a new path too. After several months of dating, they married, and they began to trust and live and love. And they invited God to strengthen them in unfamiliar territory.

So far it is going pretty good. I know that because this is the story of my husband and me.

The empowering discovery of taking a journey into your past is that you have the knowledge to alter your future. You see the places in your life where you've acquired negative behaviors, and you can lose the ones you don't want to keep. Looking at what has come through your genealogy, you can see why your neurons fire the way they do, and you can apply this knowledge to set new patterns that you can practice and pass on.

By taking up your courage and looking through the rear view lens, you may be the one to break an unhealthy chain. And your children and children's children will bless you for it.

Looking at Your Memories Builds Hope

She had green eyes, brown hair, and a soul that far surpassed her years. I loved her immediately. On the day we met, her father brought her to my apartment with the goal that she would approve of his choice. His intentions with me were becoming serious, and her approval would be paramount for his decision to move ahead. We ate pizza, I was nervous, and she looked at a painting on my wall and said, "That makes me feel peaceful." I smiled, hoping she would feel the same about me.

Because she fiercely loved her dad, she opened her heart wide to me, and when we got engaged, I was thrilled at the prospect of being her mom. There was enough room for two moms in this little girl's heart, and I basked in her generosity. We shopped and baked cookies, sang and played games, and I learned my way into a child's love. She was the gift my engagement brought me, and not having a child of my own made this gift even more precious. She taught me the dance of a stepmother's love—how it needs to know its place to move at its best. I learned to give her space so our love could safely grow.

When my engagement fell apart, I wasn't sure if my heart broke more over her or her dad, but the chasm I was left with was big enough for both. I remember wondering what to do with a God who fills your heart and then empties it, leaving you with a wider gap than the one you previously had. For a time I felt overlooked by his grace, and wondered if I had somehow slipped out of his sight.

Five years later when I welcomed my stepson into my life, I saw with new eyes the gift that little girl was. She had come into my heart to make room for the boy who would one day take her place. Time revealed an angle on my story that I couldn't see while I was living it. The rear view lens showed me God's fingerprints where I never imagined they'd be.

Looking back on our stories, we discover that some of them acquire new meaning with time, and those stories become shaped by our perspective. We have only to reflect on our past with knowledge we now have to realize that some things are not what we thought they were. When we're conscious of this fact we can be aware, while we are living our story, that it may be viewed differently with time. This fills us with hope in the midst of a difficult season, because we realize that what we see now may not be all there is to see. The rear view gives us the filter we need to know we are not seeing our circumstances for all they are.

Looking back can also give us strength to move forward in our faith. For that reason, God often prompts us to look back at what's happened in order to gain courage for what is ahead. Scripture affirms this truth; there are many stories in the Bible where we can summarize God's guidance in a single word: *remember*. The Israelites built stone altars to remind them where God had met them (Gen 13:18; 28:18; 33:20) and sang songs to remember the miracles that occurred (Ex 15). Throughout the Old Testament, God's encouragement to remember whispers to us in the stories we read, and we should make it a practice to remember the stories we live. Our memories can strengthen our hope.

Stories of faith remind us of what's true about God's love when we can't see our way ahead. When we look through the rear view mirror, we are reminded who we are—and how loved we've been—and this gives us confidence to hold on to our faith no matter what we face. Our stories can strengthen us in our fears and help us wait out dark times when things look bleak. They inspire us to know that God is with us, even when it feels like he's nowhere to be found.

> Stories of faith remind us of what's true about God's love when we can't see our way ahead.

Remembering the dark times in our story is as important as remembering the way God worked things out, for the end of the story is amplified by what precedes it. We need the dark parts of our stories to strengthen our hearts toward hope. Perhaps it is because of the importance of our stories that the Bible is more of a storybook than a guidebook. Storytelling has strengthened people's faith and given them hope since the beginning of time, and it is clear through the Scriptures that when people needed to see God, they found him in their stories. The Bible is full of accounts of desperation and deliverance, and the hope found in the way God worked in these stories fortified people in their time of need.

It was only when people forgot their stories that they lost their way.

TELEPHONE IN THE WILDERNESS

For days they lived on the parting of the Red Sea. The picture was etched in their memory in such a way that, for a time, they could think of nothing else. For endless years they had carried the weight of how dark their story had been, and this event changed everything. Now they had a new and fuller story to pass on: a story that began in hardship but ended in glory. They had witnessed a miracle, and they were careful to take note of every detail as they walked through the walls of the sea. They sang about it, memorized it, and repeated every scene—reminding their children and children's children to pass the story on after they were gone.

This was the way of the Israelite community: their stories held their faith. They didn't just speak their stories, they breathed them through rituals and ceremonies, fasts and celebrations. Telling their stories filtered through every aspect of their life. This epic story would continue to be repeated as time passed, and they held on to it as they wandered through the wilderness day after day. When more provision occurred in the wilderness, their story became peppered with smaller but evident inklings that God was leading their path. It seemed that God had given them all the evidence they needed to hang on to their faith.

However, as months passed, the story of the exodus started to wane in the hardship of their travel. Their memory of the Red Sea grew foggy, and the way they remembered the exodus shifted and changed. Like a game of telephone, new phrases slowly began to alter their story. Egypt became a land it never had been, and Moses somehow evolved into a tyrant, forcing them on a journey of hopelessness and despair. The words of their new cry show how far they had regressed: "If only we had died by the LORD's hand in Egypt! There we sat around pots of meat and ate all the food we wanted, but you have brought us out into this desert to starve this entire assembly to death" (Ex 16:3).

Their hopelessness in the present created a completely inaccurate picture of what their lives looked like when they were suffering as slaves. What happened? Perusing the pages of Exodus, it's easy to pass judgment on these people for not having the strength or fortitude to hold on to their story. Yet one look back at our own lives makes us know how capable we are of doing the same. We forget what we need to remember, and remember things that never were, particularly in times of fear and distress. Our emotions color our memory, and we often lose the hope that our stories have to give.

The truth is, it can be a challenge to remember the good when we have been traumatized by dark seasons. The difficulties of our past may have left us with some lingering fear, and we can build on that fear when we are in current seasons of struggle. Fear not only has the power to filter what happened in our past; it can prevent us from having faith in present circumstances. If we don't grab hold of the hope in our past stories, we may even *create* a bad ending for our future just so we won't be surprised. This is what happened to the Israelites in the wilderness. They stopped remembering God's deliverance at the sea and became so afraid to lose their lives in the wilderness that their fears led them into a self-fulfilling prophecy. Remembering the hope of our stories could be a more important journey than we thought.

Thankfully, our brains have been designed in such a way that enables us to rise to this challenge. When we take a closer look at that design, we discover how we can hold on to hope.

THE MYTH OF THE MEMORY BANK

If you're like me, you may have imagined your memory as a safe deposit box—something you access when you want to think about the past, which you find unchanged every time you return. But the truth is, there is no such thing as a memory bank. Every time you remember something, the memory itself changes, because your current mental process is having an influence on the way you think. The setting you are in and the feelings you are experiencing can shape the memory you are having.

You may have thought the way you remember your life story was irrevocably chiseled in granite, but you have more power to shape your memory than you thought. As Curt Thompson explains, when we are remembering the past, we are activating a particular set of neural networks. As these networks are fired, they create an awareness of a past event or anticipated future, but *our brain activity is taking place only in the present moment.* For that reason, no past is set in stone, because the way we access and remember that past is happening *right now.* With this knowledge, we realize we are empowered to shape a memory by the way we choose to remember it.

This is tremendously hopeful because we can see the power we have in our present lives for how our memories get shaped. We can't change the facts of our past, but we can and do alter our memory of it. Your past on its own does not have the ability to highjack your current or future hope. Unless, of course, your memory lets it.

A STORY OF MEMORIES GONE BAD

The time finally came for the Israelite community to end their travels in the wilderness. They stood on the edge of the land God gave them, and all they had to do was go in and get it. To prepare for this new and anticipated future, Moses sent twelve spies to scout out the land.

When the spies returned, their report began with a benign observation about what they saw: the land was good, the people were powerful, and the cities were fortified. However, reading the account, you can observe how their memory began to be shaped. Within sentences, they minimized the accessibility of the land and maximized the size of the people living in it. As their fear escalated, their report turned into a fantasy—the people were giants, the land was man eating, and the Israelites would be devoured if they returned (Num 13:27-33). Passing their fear onto the community, their story of defeat got written before it ever took place. Sadly, it was because of the influence of this altered memory that their future became exactly what they envisioned it would be.

However, nestled within this account there are two spies who remembered the land differently. Caleb and Joshua saw the land as good for the taking, and they tried to subdue the negative voices to stay focused on who God had proven himself to be. Because they were able to hold on to the hope of their memory, Joshua and Caleb ended up being the only ones who experienced what God wanted all of them to have (Num 14:26-38). Where they focused in their memory determined the strength of their faith.

> The way we remember our stories *can* actually alter our future.

We see from this account that the way we remember our stories *can* actually alter our future. If we only remember the dark parts without remembering God's faithfulness, our future choices will be directed by our fear rather than our faith. For that reason, we need to pay attention to how our memories are shaped.

MUSCLE MEMORY

My stepson is a musical prodigy. At this point, we are not sure what he will do with it, but since I have no biology invested you can trust me in this assessment. He just has that musical knack. My husband is a musician, so he is able to appreciate the nuances of his talent. I just enjoy being entertained. However, there was one day when I was not enjoying being entertained, because the keyboard in his room was playing when there was supposed to be studying going on. When I walked in, I found him doing his homework with one hand while reaching back to the keyboard and playing a song with another. His eyes were focused on his workbook while he played a song by Adele.

"What are you doing?" I asked.

"Muscle memory," he replied.

"Well, I have another memory for you. The one where we said, 'Before you do anything else, get your homework done first.'"

"But Mom, the whole point of muscle memory is you are supposed to play while you do something else, so that your muscles learn to move that way without thinking about it. Then it becomes automatic."

The boy was onto something here. After directing him back to his singular task of homework, I left the room and started thinking about what he said. The truth is, muscle memory can be used for more than just music; it can be used to build our faith. The more we practice remembering the faith aspects of our stories, the more naturally they come into view. The opposite is also true. Sharpening our focus to notice God's faithfulness requires practice before it becomes something we automatically do.

Looking back on our stories, we can always find hope—if we've trained our eyes to look for it. But this requires being open to *how* that hope might have come. It may be that hope came from something we were kept from that left us grateful, or something we were given that became more than we dreamed. Time alters and builds on our stories, and we may need to hold on to what the story *became* to hold on to our hope.

However, it is important to note that not all of our sufferings are turned into blessings. Hope can also be found through what happened *in* us when something was resolved differently than we had hoped. Sometimes hope is revealed in the way our pain has moved us toward a bigger life: an unanswered prayer made room for another person's need, or suffering we endured brought empathy for someone else's hardship. These glimpses of hope require highly trained eyes and a mature faith, for God's ways may *include* our sacrifice. Sometimes we look back and see God *in* our pain rather than in how our pain was removed.

Looking back also gives us reason to hope in the present, for we remember that what we see right now is not the full story of what is happening. The rear view reveals that time will offer us a different angle to what we currently see. Some of the things we pray for and do not get may be making room for something we will eventually need. We may not know what that is for a time, but

> In community we are reminded that God is at work in the stories around us, and that can encourage us when we don't see him in our own.

waiting is part of the journey of faith. We cannot *grow* our faith if we never *live* by faith—and God is invested in giving us that opportunity.

Training our eyes to see God's movement also shows us the importance of having a community of faith. In community we are reminded that God is at work in the stories around us, and that can encourage us when we don't see him in our own. When challenges and discouragements overwhelm us, we need other voices to remind us who God is and what he is able to do. Without the perspective of others, even the best of us can lose our hope.

REMEMBERING AGAIN

He came upon a tree, sat down under it, and prayed that he might die. The greatness of yesterday's event had dimmed under the threat of a much smaller challenge, and now he hardly remembered the heroic faith he had displayed. Because of the stress of his journey, it's not hard to imagine how Elijah's mind turned the way it did. Perhaps it was exhaustion smattered with memory loss, but after his amazing showdown of the gods, Elijah's hope had been disintegrated by a single female voice. Suicidal and depressed, he cowers in a cave under her threat.

Without anyone to remind him where he's been or what has happened, Elijah has forgotten what God can do. The weight of his current discouragement has altered his perspective. As he sits alone in a cave, God sends an angel to feed him and give him rest. However, it's what God says to him outside of that cave that restores Elijah back to his former state of hope.

Out of thin air, God speaks: "What are you doing here, Elijah?"

Feeling comforted by the voice, Elijah recounts his story: how all the prophets have been put to death and he is the only one left, and now the queen is after him to kill him too. There is no mention of the great showdown of the gods that just occurred, no mention of Elijah's giant victory. The past success has blurred in his present discouragement, and just like the Israelites in the wilderness, Elijah's current state of mind has created a new and despairing story.

So a second time, in a gentle whisper, the voice asks him the same question: "What are you doing here, Elijah?"

Elijah repeats his despairing story, and the story remains unchanged. At this point the voice says something worth pondering: "Go back the way you came." A loose paraphrase might be, "Elijah, I'm sending you back to remember what actually happened, not what you are currently remembering about what happened."

How will Elijah do that? Three people are named by God who will come alongside Elijah, and they will help restore his memory. God seems to know that Elijah is not equipped on his own to remember everything about his faith and his hope. In community Elijah will be reminded who God is, and that will strengthen his mind and heart for a different future than the one he currently has in mind (see 1 Kings 19).

Looking back on his story *in the presence of others* who affirm his faith, Elijah will remember why he has hope.

And when we look back on our stories with our community of faith, so will we. In the company of others, we can remember our faith stories in a way we cannot remember alone. And when we do that, we mark a path of faith for those who follow us after we are gone.

STONES TO REMIND US OF OUR STORIES

The first time I caught a glimpse of a small pile of stones on a trailhead, I vaguely noticed them. When I saw this marking a second time, I realized they had been strategically placed. A small pile of stones was the ecofriendly way of saying, "Go this way, not that way." In blazing new trails as a hiker, I learned to appreciate their help.

Perhaps in that same spirit, I referenced at the beginning of this chapter the Old Testament practice of people building stone altars to trace their journey of faith. When God met them in a certain place, they placed stones on their path, which reminded those who traveled after them that something happened in that place. Throughout Israel, piles of stones reminded the Israelite community that God was with them and working in their midst. I discovered when I went to Israel thousands of years later, that some of those stones have been excavated to help us retrace our stories of faith.

Stone altars were used to anchor the great stories of faith so people could remember what happened in that place. It was a way to remind the community of the generations of God's faithfulness, when people were struggling to find their way. Small piles of stones fortified their courage on present trails and enabled them to move forward in faith.

However our "stones" take shape, they can be that for us too. Whether these stones take shape in our journals or our songs, our books or our art, they can be tangible expressions of the stories we live that can bring us hope. Through them we are able to see the importance of the rear view lens in strengthening and clarifying the journey ahead.

What might those stones look like for you?

LENS 4

THE HIGHER VIEW

*Look at everything always as though
you were seeing it either for the first
or last time: Thus is your time
on earth filled with glory.*

**BETTY SMITH,
"A TREE GROWS IN BROOKLYN"**

8

Pausing to Notice God's Gifts

Skimming through a devotional called *The Reflective Life* (oxymoron noted), I stumbled upon these words: "It's a great loss that we awake to so many gifts on a given day, not only without opening them, but without knowing they are even there for us to open."

There, in the middle of the page, the words grew bold. I think it was because I recognized their truth. As a parent I am uncomfortably aware that "filling our lives up" gradually becomes our job description. It begins with soccer and homework, and ends with overtime and stress. You don't even have to be a parent to count the amount of times you hear the word *busy* on any given day. We are like the rabbit in *Alice in Wonderland*, scurrying around to our "very important dates," while a still, small voice whispers to us that we are missing things that could turn out to be most important of all. We have to *stop* in order to listen to the voice, because it is calling us to a lens that requires something from us to give us its view: our attention.

Selah is a Hebrew word we find in the Old Testament. In English this word generally means, "take a pause." We find this word repeated in the margins of the psalms, strategically placed at the end of an important thought. The psalmist inserts it when he wants us to think about what we just read. *Look at that again,* the word says, *See what's there.*

Seems to me, we could use a little *selah* in our lives.

I don't know if you've noticed, but we seem to be evolving into a pauseless generation. With limitless opportunities for communication and entertainment, we are now able to fill every second of our lives. But somewhere in the deep recesses of our soul, we have an awareness that the best parts of our lives don't happen in our overfilled moments. The best parts happen when we *selah* and take life in—when we really *look* at the people in front of us and are open to see what each day brings.

In the space of those moments, we are positioned before the lens of the higher view. And one of the things we discover through this lens is that God has placed gifts all around us that are waiting to be seen. Our task is to open our eyes so we can see them.

GIFTS IN PASSING

I was in the checkout line grabbing some groceries. He was perched in a stroller behind me, squealing with delight. I had to turn around to see what in the world had captured this baby's attention. Searching the angle of his eyes, I discovered what he saw: the entrance to the store.

Every time the sliding door opened, the baby cheered when someone entered the store. As I watched I suddenly had an urge to cheer with him. Smiles swept across the faces of the checkout line, and for a moment we were all carried into his celebration. Every person who entered the store felt like they had won an award.

The baby didn't know enough to realize entering a store was not worth cheering about. Or maybe we didn't know enough to realize it was. A voice within nudged me—this baby was showing us something. He was cheering as if he saw the stories we could not see. Because there is a story behind every person who enters a store. Some are full-time caregivers for aging parents; others are working three jobs just to feed their kids. Some may be three days in to battling an addiction; still others face battlegrounds in their homes. We may have just walked by someone who has been told that they (or someone they love) have three months left to live.

If we could see into each other's lives, we would all be cheering. Because we would see people around us who exhibit courage just by getting up. Looking back, I think God made that baby the grocery greeter. And God placed him in line behind me to whisper some perspective into my life. I left that store seeing people different from when I walked in.

It was just a simple gift of a moment, given to me by a baby. One I would have missed had I not stopped to look. But it made me wonder how many moments have happened that I *haven't* seen. Gifts God had for me if only I had slowed down long enough to see them. *Selah* makes room for the spiritual lens God has given us to truly see.

THE GIFT OF REORDERED TIME

While in college I worked at a Christian bookstore where I used to peruse the racks of those ninety-nine-cent perfect-for-a-college-budget booklets. One stood out from the rest because the title was in all capital letters. It almost seemed to scream for my attention when I walked by the rack. It was called *The Tyranny of the Urgent*.

In a nutshell, the booklet proclaimed that the greatest danger in life is "letting the urgent crowd out the important." The rest of the little book describes what exactly that phrase means. The things we *say* are important to us—spending time with our child, helping someone who has a need, deepening our most important relationships—get pushed aside by urgent "lesser" tasks that demand our immediate attention. Deadlines, projects, appointments, meetings, these are what consume our days. Because these things scream incessantly with their demands, they often leave us with no time for anything else. However, I have to say what I found most interesting in this little book were these words—delivered, perhaps, in a moment of unknown prophecy: "The telephone breaches the walls with imperious demands. The momentary appeal of these tasks seem irresistible and important, and they devour our energy."

Charles Hummel wrote this book in the 1960s, when telephones were still attached to our walls. I can't help but wonder how he would describe the "breaching of telephone walls" today. As I write, our phones have the capability of consuming our entire lives. We text, we talk, we game, we search, we order, we watch, and we record. If this book stays in print, some of you will have phones that don't just consume your lives, they may even have the capability of living them. It appears that upcoming generations are gradually disappearing into their telephone screens while missing out entirely on the people in their midst. Today, I battle that truth in my own son.

But the principle of this tyranny is the same, no matter what culture it comes in: we need to consciously *stop* if we want to take more of life in. Slowing down helps us live. I have always been struck by the fact that grandparents and children share such a special bond; perhaps that is because they share the same pace of life. Too young or old to have much of an agenda, they respond to what's next on their path. What is interesting is that the most influential person in history left his carpentry business and made "responding to what was on his path" his job description. Opening the New Testament, we discover that many of Jesus' encounters appeared to be happenstance. Jesus spent most of his time in conversations with people who crossed his path. Yet with each encounter, whether it was spontaneous or planned, Jesus found reason enough to pause, even when people around him were pushing him where they felt he needed to be. While heading to one place, he would often make room for another story, and this merely made the story he was in even greater (see, for example, Lk 8:40-54). What would our life be like if we saw our moments the same way?

The truth is, many of God's best gifts come packaged in inconvenience. We have to see beyond the disruption to receive what they have to give. But when we look back, we discover some of our detours have brought us gifts we never would have had if the interruption had not taken place. Looking at those detours differently is what the higher view encourages us to do.

> Many of God's best gifts come packaged in inconvenience.

GIFTS IN INTERRUPTIONS

Glancing up from the computer, I looked for what was making that unfamiliar noise. It was 6:30 a.m., and I had started a load of laundry to get ready for our next day's trip. "Thud, thud, thud" the washer banged, loud enough to distract me from seeing the growing flood on our bathroom carpet. When I finally looked down at the carpet, I heard some words come out of my mouth that were unfamiliar to my vocabulary.

My husband continued on his own string of those words as he attempted to Shop-Vac the carpet and waylay the impending mold. Then he left to go to work. I stared at the mountain of clothes that I was somehow supposed to get done by the end of the day.

Gathering myself together, I left to get our boy to school with the cookies I had baked for the school party. Trying to be a good witness to the mom who was in charge, I attempted the calm and humorous approach as I recapped the morning's events. "Why don't you just come over and do your laundry at my place?" she offered, paling my "good witness" with her kind words. I hardly knew her, so I politely declined. The last thing I wanted was to inconvenience her the first time we met. Three hours later with no repairman in sight and visions of spending my already filled up day at the laundromat, I texted her. "You know, if you're really okay with this . . ." She texted me back immediately that she was. I loaded my huge pile of wet clothing in the back of my car and headed to her door.

Five hours of in-and-out conversations later, my new friend, Audrey, began sharing her heart. When she found out I worked at a church, she told me her son wanted to be Jesus for Halloween. (My son attends church every week, and I can say that particular choice of costume has never come up.) Understandably, she had a few questions about her son's budding spirituality.

Turns out, the Sunday before, her son had actually asked her to take him to church. Five days and a broken washing machine later, I showed up at her door. "There seems to be something bigger going on here," I offered, beginning to suspect God was in this interruption for more than just my hassle. Three months later, as I watched Audrey and her family find a home in our church, I wondered what would have happened if my washing machine had worked. Certainly all the events could have unfolded in a similar way, but I wouldn't have had the privilege of being a part of it. A broken washing machine gave me that gift.

Some gifts come wrapped to feel like liabilities, interruptions to the path we have in mind. But when we look back, those gifts often turn out to be the best gifts of all. They may not be ones we are looking for, and they may be different from the gifts we seek. But when we are open to receive what comes our way, we may discover some of our gifts work their way into our lives in ways we can't imagine. And sometimes the gifts that come wrapped in packages we'd never choose turn out to be the best of all.

THE HARDEST AND BEST GIFTS

Prior to her third child's birth, she'd overheard her husband wishing they had tried for another child. When Patty discovered she was pregnant, she was thrilled to give him his wish. Finding out it was a boy made their joy complete. The emergency C-section made his arrival more dramatic than she had planned, but when she saw his perfect face, her fears melted with relief. With two doting big sisters and adoring parents, this baby was the prize that would make their family just what she dreamed it would be.

When Leyton turned two, Patty began to see some things in him that were different. His growth steps were not matching other babies his age. However, at all of her doctor's appointments, the phrase, "Let's just see what happens," was the verdict she continued to hear. When Leyton began having periodic seizures, Patty was done hearing that verdict. She and her husband laid awake at night terrified that his breathing would stop. As days and months passed, they moved blindly forward, having no idea what was to come.

When Leyton started school, they were able to manage the seizures through medication, and Patty hired speech therapists and special ed teachers to try to help him keep up. However, it soon became clear that "keeping up" was not going to be Leyton's path. The growth of his body made the difference in his cerebral development more apparent, but somehow in the middle of that disparity, his heart and spirit grew biggest of all. In the ongoing drama of Leyton's unfolding life, the one person who remained untouched by it all was Leyton.

When Patty's research led her to put him in a rigorous program that required a highly restricted diet and monitored breathing exercises, Leyton's spirit remained unbroken. The first Halloween after he began, Patty's heart sunk when she saw all the candy he'd collected that he could not eat. Silently she watched him, as he combed through his mountain of treats and joyfully held up the one lone bag of Skittles his diet allowed. As he beamed at her, Patty recognized again what she already knew: Leyton's eyes were different than her own. And through them, she began to see her own life differently.

Patty came to see that the sorrows she had for Leyton were not sorrows he had for himself, and she began to wonder whether he was the disadvantaged one. When people ate food he couldn't have, Leyton chewed on his vegetables and fruit. When other kids were not secure enough to play with him, he found ways to entertain himself. When Patty and her husband worried about Leyton's future, his focus was on what came next. His mere presence in a room often caused others around him to recognize their own disabilities. They were just hidden and less apparent.

Perhaps the greatest irony is that Leyton has done more for Patty's life than she has done for his—and through him, she is being transformed. She wakes up each day looking at what's in front of her, because his perspective prohibits her from focusing on what's to come. She is more generous with the grace she gives to others, because it's all she ever sees moving through her son. The half-empty cup she is prone to see turns half-full with the vision he gives her. He has called out her best, and in so doing has captured her heart.

The mystery of God's greatest gifts is that they come in packages we'd never ask for, and they require more from us than we think we have. But these gifts bring a joy greater than we ever imagined there could be. They are an indicator that there is a Giver who knows us better than we know ourselves. And he is also writing a story that is bigger than we can see.

Recently, Leyton made a friend at church. The boy was new, and when the teacher observed his warmth, she asked the boy if he wanted to be Leyton's special friend. They spent the Sunday school hour reading and playing games, and both boys loved their time together. Later that week, the new boy's mother received a note extolling her son's kindness to Leyton. The mother was touched but not completely surprised. Just a couple months earlier, her son had told her he wanted to be Jesus for Halloween— he just decided to do it without dressing up. And if you are wondering whether a broken washing machine was ever involved in this story, you are a very smart reader.

In order for our hands to receive life's gifts, we often have to let go of what we're holding in them. And for most of us that requires ongoing work. Expectations and agendas don't die easily, and

> In order for our hands to receive life's gifts, we often have to let go of what we're holding in them.

sometimes we cling to them until they are pried from our hands. But when we see what comes in their place, we wonder why we didn't let go more easily, because the least likely packages often contain the very best gifts.

OPENING OUR HANDS

"I think you two should meet each other," the chaplain said, and I turned to see a blonde woman my height standing by the door. The chaplain knew the Marine life was new to me, and he thought it might be good for me to meet someone whose husband would soon be deployed. We said a brief hello and made a date to have coffee after her husband and my fiancé left for Iraq.

Driving to the coffee shop, I remember wanting to know her Marine wife secrets—how she lived without her husband for so many months. This would soon be my life, and I needed to see how she survived. I wanted to learn how she toggled between single parenting and sharing the load, managing her fears, while calming her children's, helping with homework and attending school plays, driving to sports commitments, and enduring endless dinners alone. I thought teaching me about the life she had would be the gift she would bring to mine.

Many months and meals later, my friend Melissa stood by me when my Marine engagement ended. Five years later she stood at the altar as a bridesmaid with me when I became a different man's wife. Somewhere between laughter and dinners out, walks and shared secrets, her wisdom for what I thought my life would be and holding my faith for what she believed would still come, the two of us forged a friendship that lasted beyond my broken engagement. She was the gift this season had brought me, expanding the purpose my broken engagement had for my life. The circumstances of our meeting showed me that some

things start out one way and end up being another thing altogether. But if we keep our hands open, there are always gifts.
And sometimes the gifts that come in our least desired packages
turn out to be dearest of all.

Perhaps in that same spirit we can look with fresh eyes at the
circumstances in front of us. If we know God gives good gifts,
even if some appear to be liabilities, we can trust that we will
eventually discover the good they bring. These gifts may not
have been what we asked for, or may have come in a package that
is different than we hoped, but if we believe that the Giver is
good, we can trust that they are somehow exactly what we need.

Jesus unveils a greater understanding of God's gifts when he
asks, "Which of you, if your son asks for bread, will give him a
stone? Or if he asks for a fish, will give him a snake? . . . How
much more will your Father in heaven give good gifts to those
who ask him!" (Mt 7:9-11). Notice that we are *not* promised we'll
get what we ask for; we are promised that what we get will be
good. And the longer we pause to look at God's gifts, the more
we discover that truth.

When we are open to what lies in front of us, we find more
gifts to receive. Because our gifts unfold through our moments.
So we wait and watch. As Thomas Kelly reminds us, "God
himself works in our souls, taking increasing control as we are
progressively willing to be prepared for His wonder." And as we
lift our eyes, we see the earth is full of his gifts.

9

Seeing the Purpose for Your Pain

Just a day before, she was wondering how she would pay for her groceries. Now all she could think about was sending her children down a sex-trafficking path for water to drink. She knew something big was stirring in her soul. Chrissie and her husband had been forced to sublease their bedroom because of sudden unemployment, but hearing the visitor speak in church about these desperate mothers put her trouble in a whole new light. The sacrifices she was currently having to make grew strangely pale as he continued to speak.

She'd been moved by stories of poverty before, but this one reached beyond her sympathy and lodged inside her gut. As the man spoke about the need for clean water in the Congo, hearing about Congolese mothers sending their children down dangerous paths pierced her heart. Their plight caused her to see her own struggle with new eyes. But when she heard what it would cost to give an entire family clean water *for life*, she wasn't prepared for how the volume turned up in her soul.

Fifty dollars.

The amount she needed for two days' worth of groceries was all each family needed to have water for life. Our church watched as Chrissie led a marathon team to help raise that money. Initially the idea of raising money seemed ludicrous to her, when she had such a need herself. Ironically, it was that very need that led her to sign up. Somehow she deeply connected with the plight of these mothers—and with their pain inside her she felt her own pain differently. She began to see her story through a different lens.

Two years and $145,000 later, our church's marathon team provided three thousand Congolese families with clean water for life. Chrissie eventually passed the baton to another young mom who took over as team leader when Chrissie got a full-time job. Between the two of them, and the teams they recruited, the amount they raised over a three-year period was $250,000. Five thousand Congolese families now have water for life.

Chrissie knows that if she had not gone through what she did, she might not have been moved to do what she's done. And for that reason she is grateful for her difficulty. Paul writes in 2 Corinthians 1:4 that God "comforts us in all our troubles, so that we can comfort those in any trouble," but this only happens when we let trouble take us on its path. Chrissie was able to understand on a visceral level the fear of not being able to provide for her kids. And through Chrissie's willingness to let her pain be used, God answered those mothers' prayers.

This high calling is the gift that Chrissie's difficulty brought to her. But it only evolved as it did because of what she allowed her difficulty to help her see. Chrissie's story illustrates that there is a purpose in our pain that can broaden our story more than we could ever conceive. The higher view lens helps us recognize how our pain can be used.

THE STORY WE'VE BEEN GIVEN TO LIVE

Your wounds carry a distinctive ministry because others need what you alone have. At any given moment, you can move from a chapter of pain and brokenness to a chapter of healing and strength by seeing your pain in the context of a bigger story. When you find a purpose for your pain, it not only helps you move through it in a healthy way, but as you reach out you discover that your pain is uniquely designed to help others.

> At any given moment, you can move from a chapter of pain and brokenness to a chapter of healing and strength by seeing your pain in the context of a bigger story.

I saw evidence of this one morning as I glanced at the news and saw a young woman being interviewed in Los Angeles. She was standing next to a church where I used to volunteer in an afterschool program for inner-city kids. The young woman, Latrina, had become a ward of the state when she was two years old. She had been moved from a foster home to a group home to eventual emancipation when she turned eighteen, and her bio sounded like a recipe to become exactly what her drug-addicted mom modeled for her to be. Instead, Latrina was able to navigate the way through her pain to become something else.

With the support of friends and several organizations, Latrina was able to find a job and a home. But instead of leaving her pain behind her, she found a way to encourage others who were experiencing her plight. As a child she remembered her grandmother's sweet potato pie comforted her in her challenges, so a dream was planted to use that recipe to encourage others. Soon the vision of "Sweet Tri Pastries" was born.

Once a month Latrina sets up a table on Skid Row to hand out free sweet potato pie and pastries. She delivers baked goods to foster children and battered women who are in temporary housing to spread her comfort and care. Latrina realizes this small act of kindness will not make much of a difference in the problems associated with homelessness. She just wants people struggling with homelessness to know that she cares. From her own experience, she realizes a simple touch of care can make a huge difference in the trajectory of someone's life.

While I was volunteering at a church on Skid Row, I saw hundreds of kids in Latrina's circumstances. However, I never saw anyone go on to live their story of homelessness the way she did. The fact that she was able to let her pain move through her to touch others revealed that she saw her wounds as bigger than herself. And her life is an illustration of what personal difficulty can become.

When you've experienced a specific pain, you have a unique opportunity to minister to others. But being a wounded healer requires vulnerability that lays you bare for who you are. When you understand the gift your pain can be, you can be empowered by God to take that risk. Henri Nouwen provides helpful insight when he says that we should view our pain and suffering as something shared by all of humanity: "Making one's own wounds a source of healing does not call for a sharing of superficial personal pains, but for a constant willingness to see one's own pain and suffering as rising

> Through the higher view lens, you see that your pain is for a purpose. It is meant to join with others who may be struggling on a similar path.

from the depth of the human condition which all people share." We all have pain—it just comes packaged in different wounds.

Through the higher view lens, you see that your pain is for a purpose. It is meant to join with others who may be struggling on a similar path. If you lay your pain out and let others see, they will find strength from your company. And with your willingness to let pain be used, even the darkest story can become a story of hope.

THE STORY THAT'S IN US TO HEAL

When the story broke, I was more than shocked; the news ripped into my ears and tore my heart. I couldn't put together the person my pastor had been to me and the things he had done. I had to work through my own grief before I could fathom the fallout of those nearer to him. His marriage had been the envy of all of us—we were college age and fresh faced, and he and his wife stood before us as an aspiration of what we all wanted to be. Hearing the news of his affairs and abuse during that time caused a piece of my heart to be broken that would never be put back the same.

Months after the story came out, his wife and I walked on a beach together, mostly in silence. Along with the personal devastation she endured, one of the greatest heartaches of the story was finding out that her sister was one of her husband's victims.

Forced to live in denial for most of her young adult years, Susie remembers thinking her brother-in-law's advances were wrong at first. But his power and persuasion outweighed her resolve to keep him away. Slowly she developed a dual personality that enabled her to survive. Toggling between her role as the younger sister, pure and innocent, and the role she played with her sister's husband, who kept her under his control, she hid the truth deep inside, hoping it would eventually disappear. Her brother-in-law even attempted to direct her in who and when she would marry, but under God's providence, Susie's husband turned out to be a stellar choice. The way they were able to heal their marriage after uncovering Susie's abuse was nothing short of miraculous.

Even more miraculous was what happened to Susie's life after her abuse ended. As she developed the courage to share her story, others approached her with their own stories; and she was able to reach through her wounds to offer the kind of comfort only possible because of what she had survived. The very thing she had tried to keep hidden became what others needed most, and she began to realize the gift that her story could become. Joining with other victims of abuse, she became a part of a ministry called "Day of Brave," where women could meet and share their stories. They found that by sharing stories, and the strength that came with them, healing could be found.

Now a young grandmother, Susie's ministry to victims of abuse has traveled beyond her immediate area and extends to the country of Belize. After visiting there on a mission trip, she saw that incest and abuse transcended cultures, and she knew that the secrets kept wounded people most. As Susie began to share her story, she inspired other women to do the same, and they discovered the freedom that came by speaking their shame. Today, in her small town in Washington, she runs a lay counseling ministry for women moving toward healing from abuse.

If given the chance to pray it away, Susie would have taken it with her story. Yet she realizes she has been given an opportunity for ministry with her courage to give it away. Susie's experience of pain and brokenness has been rewritten to become a story of healing and hope—because she broke through her shame and allowed her pain to be used. Today there are women whose lives have been transformed because of Susie's choice.

The story of the woman at the well in John 4 illustrates a similar truth; her encounter with Jesus led her to share her hidden secrets in a very public way. When she goes back to her town, she says, "Come, see a man who told me everything I ever did" (Jn 4:29). We can only imagine the follow-up conversations: "And what exactly did you do?" The Samaritan woman's willingness to open up the dark closet of her life and speak her truth in such a transparent way reveals the healing she experienced from Jesus. And because of her testimony, she is the first to extend the reach of Jesus' love.

When we've been healed from a season of deep pain, we are often tempted to leave it behind us. The mystery of the higher view reveals there can be a greater healing when we hold a piece of it to give away. When we look at the final chapter of Jesus' earthly ministry, we discover that mystery may just be God's intent.

SENT WITH BLESSINGS AND WOUNDS

In 2 Corinthians 1:5, Paul writes, "Just as we share abundantly in the sufferings of Christ, so also our comfort abounds through Christ." And in one of the final scenes after Jesus' resurrection, we are given a deeper glimpse into that truth. Three days after Jesus' death, his closest friends are huddled together. Rumors have been swirling over his reappearance, but the disciples have been hidden away, nursing their grief. Everything they knew was not what they thought it was, and in the wake of his death on the cross, they felt empty and alone.

Suddenly through the locked door, the resurrected Jesus appeared before them. And into their frightened souls, he proclaimed his first word, "Peace." Showing them the wounds in his hands and his side, he speaks to them about their calling with these words: "As the Father has sent me, I am sending you" (Jn 20:21).

Reading it quickly, we assume Jesus' commission is simply to tell others about his resurrection. It seems the disciples are simply called to bless others with the hope of new life. However, the context of the passage reveals that Jesus says these words after he shows them his wounds. And I wonder, with this awareness, could Jesus' words be read another way? "As the Father sent me, *with my wounds*, so I send you *with yours*." Reading it this way, it's possible we get a window into the way God sends us.

Prior to this passage, Jesus uses his wounds to give proof of the resurrection. But in holding his pierced hands out before he commissions the disciples, he leaves room for us to see our wounds as part of our call. This is the ministry that the higher view opens our eyes to see.

THE STORY WE HOLD ON TO FOR OTHERS

The first year after their son's death was the hardest year for them to go through. They had been there with him, and were not sure they could handle their immense grief. When the time came to sign up for the camp, they realized it was exactly where they needed to be.

In the first six months of Zach's life, he had been under anesthesia thirty times. But it had all been worth it on the day the doctor pronounced their baby cancer free. As they watched first steps get taken and a vibrant personality form, their hopes soared; however, with the cancer Zach had inherited, they knew that they were always a diagnosis away from its return.

In Zach's ninth year, the thing they feared most reared its ugly head. It became evident something was wrong when he suddenly went blind. For one year, Zach learned to live with his new limitation like a champ while he went through ten months of chemotherapy to get rid of the tumors that were starting to spread. After his treatments were through, Doug and Laurie received an invitation to attend a camp for families battling cancer. Weighing the challenges, it was where their family needed to be.

After they returned home, Zach lived just four more months. He died on Christmas Eve in a hospital room, surrounded by those who loved him most. The pain that shot through Doug and Laurie's heart struck up permanent residence that day, and they discovered with each passing year it would always have a room in the middle of their souls.

The following year when they were asked to come back to the camp, their pain cried out a resounding no! However, given some time to think about it, they gave their daughter the deciding vote. Her yes steered their course, and though their wounds were raw and in tact, they knew when they got there it was exactly where they needed to be. Without Zach, their roles shifted to supporting other families, and in this new role they experienced the healing of pain being used. Somehow as their pain moved out, it changed, and while it was no less difficult to endure, it held a mysterious fulfillment.

Each year they go back to serve, they feel the familiar dread when they pack their bags. Each year when they return, they are filled in a way that can only be explained supernaturally. During their stay, they are able to sit with parents of terminal kids in a way that no one else can. Doug and Laurie have resolved to walk through their grief rather than around it, for they know that is the only way to survive in their story. And because of their courage, others have experienced healing by what their sadness has become.

"As the Father has sent me, I am sending you," Jesus says, holding out his hands to his disciples (Jn 20:21). A week later, he shows his wounds to Thomas, and then tells Peter he'll be led where he will not want to go.

It appears that in the final scenes of Jesus' time on earth, there is a strong indication that our wounds are part of our calling. They were on Jesus' resurrected body for recognition, and also to remind the disciples how intrinsic the wounds were to his call.

And when Jesus informs Peter he will eventually be led where he doesn't want to go, he adds two words to his proclamation that we do not want to miss: "Follow me."

Because of these words from Jesus, we know we can find comfort in his companionship when we are led that way too.

Opening Your Eyes to Need

The streets were lined with poverty in every form: gray-haired, toothless women holding their wares, children with bony arms and open hands trying to catch our eyes, hungry babies dangling from distracted mothers' breasts. The smell of grilled corn, exhaust, and trash-lined streets formed a scent I came to know well in this country. But it was the small stories behind the smells that reached out and grabbed my heart.

In the distance, one woman was alone on the hill pounding two rocks together. She looked to be seventy-three, but in Haitian years, she could have been fifty. I asked my friend Ephraim what in the world she was doing. It was something very common in Haiti; she was pounding big rocks into little rocks to make a load big enough to fill a truck. It would take her two to three months if she pounded every day, and she would make seventy dollars. The day before, when I was still at home, I spent that much on a family meal.

Prior to my first visit to Haiti, I saw myself as average in my income bracket. I rented a two-bedroom apartment, drove an inexpensive car, and mostly lived check to check. When I got off the plane in Port-au-Prince, I suddenly realized I was royalty. The times I was tempted to reach for an air conditioner, water heater, or hair dryer during my stay in Haiti were too numerous to count.

As we drove through the slums of the city, I noticed that my friend Ephraim had a collection of coins in the drink holder next to him. People cried out as we drove by, and about every three blocks he would put money into the hands of someone he knew. He was something of a celebrity in Haiti; his heart and generosity had given him a reputation that stretched way beyond the four walls of his church. And as we drove, he simply did what he felt called to do.

He was rich compared to others in his country; there were people from the United States who supported him by giving him a small portion of what they made. How easy it would have been for him to keep the money others gave him; it could have provided comforts his family would have enjoyed—a couple of shrimp to balance the daily rice and beans, a short vacation to balance endless difficult days. But the money he received turned into money he gave away, because there was always someone around him who needed it more. These were the faces he continued to invite into his heart and pocketbook.

He never made me feel guilty for being rich, in fact just the opposite. He knew what we were used to in the States and always provided comforts for us that he didn't need. On the last night of our mission trip, he arranged for us to stay at a hotel after a week of work. I begged him to join us. He stayed for a couple of hours, but couldn't bring himself to be treated for the night. His awareness of need and money was more visceral than ours; he entered in to what we agonized at from a distance. Over and over, I watched him touch what we could only watch. This was the gift his upbringing had given him.

"I know where you live my friend," he'd say disarmingly. "And I understand. You are used to the ways around you."

He'd been "where I live" a couple of times, and on his first visit I took him on a tour of some of the homes a couple miles away. "If you lived here, why would you ever want to go to Heaven?" he asked with a smile, but his words pierced my heart. And I quietly wondered about their truth.

Over the years, as Ephraim has given away money I tried to get him to keep, another truth has become apparent to me. It seems when we've experienced the agony of living without something, our compassion takes on a different shape, particularly with those who share our struggle. It may be money or a husband or children or a home, but the experience of *not* having something leaves us with an understanding that is different from those who sympathize from afar. If you've lived it, you "get it" in a different way.

When it comes to poverty, most of us have to work at "getting it," since our privileged eyes are bombarded with things that make us feel like we never have enough.

Many of us can feel poor if we focus on the wealth we don't have. I live in an area where we can't afford to buy a house, where the rent for our two-bedroom cottage is more than most mortgages, and where eleven of the richest people in the world (according to *Forbes*) live less than two miles away. My perspective on living without can get a bit skewed. I attend school functions in homes that take up an entire street, and when I come home, it's embarrassingly easy for me to look around and think, *Not enough.*

We all can read the statistics and see that 80 percent of the world's population lives on less than $10 a day. But we don't live statistics. We live what is around us where we live. Most of us have to be a bit intentional about living without to truly understand what that phrase even means. I can pat myself on the back for not owning a home and not driving an expensive car and think, *I get it*. But I don't get it. Not even close.

When we look at our life through the lens of the higher view, we see the importance of "getting it," not only for what it does in our compassion for others but what it does to the way we live. Jesus talks about money and what to do with it twenty-five times in the New Testament because it's something he wanted us to *get*. Frankly, it's a lot easier to wrestle with those verses than live them.

The simple truth is, because I was born in this country, I will never understand poverty like Ephraim. But the higher view woos me to let poverty in. To see it. Smell it. Touch it. To read Jesus' words to the rich young ruler, and try not to paraphrase it to mean something else. Because the time I spend meditating on Jesus' words, and pushing myself to spend time in poverty, usually has the effect of coloring the time I spend not in it, which is otherwise known as my everyday life.

THE COLLISION OF TWO WORLDS

Mexico is where my brush with the Majority World began. It was 1989, and the youth pastor and I began taking students on weekend trips over the border to help build houses for families living in a dump. I couldn't fathom the possibility of people actually *living* in a dump until I saw it, and I still remember the shock of seeing that first set of eyes peering out of an enormous pile of garbage. A village was living in that trash, and our leader said that by the end of the day, some of those eyes would peer out of a new house. Four slabs of wood and an aluminum roof later, I saw it happen—although *house* may have been a loose translation of the structure we actually built.

It was enough to make a family of five weep with joy, and as we held their hands and prayed, we all wept with them. Heading back over the border, our tears were still fresh, and when we arrived back home late on Sunday night, our bathrooms, stoves, and mattresses took on new life and meaning. My students were left with an acute awareness that things we didn't even think about were things not everyone had. Suddenly that video game they pined for carried a lot less importance.

This is so good for them, I thought.

"Good for you too," God whispered to my heart.

It was slightly depressing to see how quickly memories fade in the light of our privileged lives. Within a week, we seemed to slip right back into what we left. I began to see that trips to witness the economical disparity of our world needed to be more than a one-time stint to do any kind of permanent work. There is something about seeing it and feeling it that motivates us differently than reading and praying about it. We are near-sighted creatures; what we have in front of us seems to suck up the greater part of our attention.

As a youth leader, I saw what mission experiences did to my students; in the most selfish season of their lives, they happily gave up their spring break to serve children whose language they didn't speak, in a place where showers and toilets were equally scarce. They cleared their calendars and begged their parents, and every year I brought them home dirtier and sicker and more alive than they'd ever been. It reminds me of the verse that in losing our lives we find them. It seems the emptier we let ourselves be, the more whole we become.

But then we come home—to our schedules and our jobs and our families and our selfishness—and we wonder how in the world to bring *that* into *this*. We try for a while, but eventually forget, and we discover with enough of these cycles that putting poverty in front of us needs to be a regular part of our everyday lives. And not just on screens.

There are places of economic disparity around us that can provide a more accessible view of poverty for those who live in this privileged country. Poverty is different in our country than in other parts of the world, as it often sits blocks away from extravagance, but it can jolt us nonetheless. Most of us can find a homeless shelter within a few miles of where we live. Need is around us in every form, and when we allow it to be in front of us, something magical happens to our eyes. The things I "need" regroup into things I "want," and the scales come off for a time, reminding me of my advantaged birth. But my heart springs back as my memory wanes, and I find I have to consistently practice putting it in front of me again. It's not a discipline I'm naturally pushed toward, but one my heart sorely needs.

> Need is around us in every form, and when we allow it to be in front of us, something magical happens to our eyes

The trick is to figure out what to do with it. Or maybe more appropriately, what it wants to do with me.

BRINGING "THAT" INTO "THIS"

One of my great temptations after I come home from a mission trip is wondering how everyone else has the gall to live the way they do. It's amazing how easy it is for me to become a mini-Mother Teresa when I reenter my privileged life. However, the amount of time it takes me to race back to my own creature comforts makes me aware that the problem isn't everyone else. I see the problem when I look in the mirror.

The fact is, I was a bit skewed in my theology in my early Christian days—with prayers of thanksgiving for all God provided *me*, and not much time thinking about what that prayer meant for everyone else. Extending my vision to include the fact that there's a bigger story going on around me, I've become aware that I have been given blessings for reasons that include more than meeting my needs. It's what to do with that knowledge that comes next.

Developing relationships with people in need puts a face and a name on poverty, and that compels us in a more personal way. Organizations like Compassion International can help "poor kids in Africa" become Jane and Joseph, and through our relationships with people in need, we bring them into our lives as an extension of our family. When "people in Haiti" become our friend Ephraim, we make him our brother and let him teach us what poverty means. When those who are born with less become a part of our family, we care for them differently. And they often bring to our lives far more than the material support we bring to theirs. We may enlarge their income, but they carry the greater ministry of enlarging our hearts.

We can also learn from those who have access to privilege and choose to live with less, living out a calling that challenges our own. Through these people we can see what it looks like when poverty gets up and moves into our lives. In my youth ministry days, one of those people was Shane Claiborne. I still remember his quiet yet pronounced descent onto our Youth Specialties conferences; he was dreadlocked and simply clothed, and spoke about taking service beyond "what was good for our students" and living it out in our everyday life. Planted among the homeless in Philadelphia, his message was fortified by how he looked, and he showed us what it was like to "live without" by choice. He

made our hair bristle and our hearts squirm because we all se-
cretly wondered if we should be doing the same.

I've noticed people like Shane get mixed results when they
speak; it's more comfortable to disagree with their message than
to let it move us to rearrange our priorities. When we inten-
tionally place the lives of people like Shane in our sightline, we
may experience an internal wrestling match within our souls.
But inward wrestling is where change begins.

Perhaps most poignantly there are those in our midst who
actually live out sacrifice right in front of us. They move us
toward need in a more visceral way, because they stand in our
view and share our lives. When we open our eyes and watch
them, we can be wooed to join them. It could be they are living
before us for exactly that purpose.

WHEN BEING MOVED MOVES OTHERS

Dennis was a youth pastor when I first met him. He was the one
who introduced me to missions in Mexico when we took our
kids to help families living in the dump. Those weekend Mexico
trips had a great influence on my future youth ministry, but they
were merely the beginning of what would unfold in his life.

Dennis didn't just do mission work on the side; he lived and
breathed it. His enthusiasm for the downtrodden was conta-
gious. Even in churches with massive wealth, he always inspired
people to give their wealth away. He was like a walking checking
account (in the very best way)—and money went to him and
through him in astoundingly large sums. However, in February
2001, a *Time* magazine cover on the AIDS crisis in Africa
reached out for more than his ability to raise funds. It leaped off
the page and grabbed his heart.

While most of us would be prompted by the article to "pray for
these people," Dennis was moved to do something else. Sharing

his passion, his wife, Susan, suggested a trip to South Africa to
see if there was anything they could do. Almost immediately after
their plane landed, they were shuttled to Cape Flats, part of
Greater Cape Town, which was an AIDS-infested, three-million-
person slum. Overwhelmed by needs too immense to take in,
they mostly listened and learned, but their broken hearts fueled
them as they headed back to the United States. After extensive
research, they found Community Health Evangelism (CHE), and
in its model they discovered a way to begin.

Knowing they would have to mobilize the community of Cape
Flats in order to make any kind of permanent dent, they were
trained in CHE and slowly learned their philosophy to achieve
positive, sustainable change. With the knowledge they gained,
they went back to Cape Town and discovered the largest problem
in the region was unemployment, so they began their work by
creating some small businesses. In the meantime, their CHE
committee uncovered untold amounts of AIDS orphans, so
Dennis and Susan began implementing youth programs to care
for and empower these kids. Eventually, plans for a boarding
school evolved, and when Bridges Academy opened, thirty orphans found their home. Since that time, sixty orphans have
graduated from Bridges and gone on to become teachers,
lawyers, nurses, and social workers. Many of those graduates
make up the teams that have trained other workers in neigh-
boring communities and countries. To date, the Bridges ministry has extended its model to Swaziland, Congo, Namibia, and
Ethiopia, so there are now five countries and tens of thousands
of people whose lives have been transformed.

It began with a magazine cover and eyes willing to see what
the pages displayed. But in truth, it began a long time before that,
when a young youth pastor led weekend Mexico mission trips

and never stopped looking for what could be done. The need he allowed himself to see eventually changed the trajectory of his life, and those of us who know him have been changed by watching him. Though most of us will never do all that God has used Dennis to do, he has been placed in our view to see what can happen with a willing heart.

WHERE TO BEGIN

Mother Teresa said, "The less we have, the more we give," which seems like a contradictory statement until you observe its truth. In my trips to Haiti, I've seen families taking in abandoned children even though they didn't have enough room for their own. I've observed people sharing food with others, not knowing when their next meal would come. Watching these dear people make these choices tells me there is profound truth to Mother Teresa's words.

Jesus' encounter with the rich young ruler illustrates the opposite truth: the more we have, the harder it is to give it away. In this disturbing encounter, Jesus meets a man who has done everything right but still feels restless in his relationship with God. Jesus sees right through to the thing he clings to—his money—and he quietly challenges the man to give it all away. The challenge is too much for the man; he cannot do it. Those of us who live in comfort and with material wealth can understand why (see Lk 18:18-25).

When I see people downsizing their lifestyles and choosing to live without, I am aware they are making a different sacrifice than my friend Ephraim, one that I find equally admirable. The willingness to partake in poverty when you don't have to live in it requires a different kind of virtue, and through the rich young ruler we see it is a virtue Jesus invites us to embrace. However, the securities we cling to can keep us from accepting his invitation, and we often miss out on the freedom that letting go can bring.

We busy ourselves and shield our eyes from need, and, sadly, we will always find people to affirm our apathy. We can distract ourselves with the thought that since we can't help that much, we might as well do nothing at all. But there is a third option, the one God consistently presents to us right

> We often miss out on the freedom that letting go can bring.

where we are. We can open our eyes to the needs around us and ask ourselves what we can do.

Wherever we are. With all our inadequacies. With whatever we let ourselves see. This is God's invitation.

JUST BEGIN

Erin always had a soft spot for the homeless. It was probably because it was her job to put people in homes. Erin was a realtor, and when she allowed herself to see the people in her community who didn't have a home, it broke her heart.

When she read a story about a Texas family that decided to serve hotdogs to the homeless, she felt a strange tugging on her heart. However, with a two year old and a four year old she needed direction to address that tugging in a way that made sense. "You see my heart," she whispered in her prayers. "Show me what you want me to see."

Within weeks, she stumbled on a feeding program called Bread of Life, which was a grassroots-led meal for the homeless that was served in a well-known park. She decided to sign up. However, the month she decided to volunteer, the program lost its leadership. A new leader needed to step up.

The timing of her prayer and the discovery of this need was too coincidental for Erin to brush aside. With no idea how she would mobilize volunteers to feed the now seventy-five homeless people who were showing up for a meal, Erin couldn't ignore the tugging in her heart. She decided to take the ministry into her hands.

Looking back, Erin knows when she took this step there were bigger hands behind hers. Each month, sometimes at the last minute, volunteers step up and bake burrito pies, put together salads, and butter bread, and this simple ministry signals to the homeless in our community that we see them. And through this small act, those of us who have gotten involved have broadened our hearts.

A couple of years ago, a group at our church was put together to explore the needs in our city. Erin joined and eventually emerged as a leader in that group. Over the last two years, a tutoring program was launched for a school with low-income families. More than fifty people from our church have stepped up and helped countless children learn to read.

Erin knew when she began opening her eyes to need that the problem of homelessness was bigger than a monthly meal. But serving that one meal is where she decided to begin. With the way her small acts have begun to shape and inspire people around her, it's anyone's guess what will happen next. But Erin's story reveals that *what we see in front of us* is the place God invites us to begin.

"We can do no great things," the great nun from Calcutta reminds us, "Only small things with great love." The higher view directs our eyes to show us where to start.

Looking at Your Life
with New Eyes

When you were born, the world changed. No one exactly like you had ever been here. A chain of events triggered your birth, and there was a specific moment when you came to be. And at that moment you became part of a story that was going on before you arrived.

Some things about your part were decided for you. You were born at a certain time, which you did not choose. Your mom and dad brought you here, and you did not get to choose who they were. You arrived at a place in the world decided without your input. And you were given a race and an ethnic heritage you did not select. These things happened outside of your control. But since then, you've been given many choices for how your life is lived.

Throughout this book you've been introduced to four lenses. I am praying they have given you a new way to see your life. But in this final chapter I want to acknowledge there may be scenes you've been given—and may be living now—that you would prefer not to live. What then?

In 2015, I watched some actors being interviewed on *Good Morning America* about their hit show, and I was struck by their comments about the process of getting their script. Because the plot line was kept a secret, the actors said they had no idea what was going to happen to them until the script was in their hands. Each Monday they would read their destiny in that particular week's show. A bad character might suddenly become good, or a good character might become bad. And at any given moment, someone might die or be sent away.

The interviewer joked, "I guess you don't want to get on the writer's bad side." They nodded and laughed. But it is what one of the actors said next that struck me most. He alluded to the fact that when they signed their contracts, whatever happened to them would be in the writers' hands. The goal was the success of the show rather than what happened in their individual scripts. The cast summarized their calling as actors by saying they may love or hate what happens to their character, but the reason they are there is for the good of the show.

Suddenly through their words, I saw a window into life.

Whatever our specific beliefs, most of us see that we are a part of a bigger story. The difference between us and the actors is that we don't get to see our script in advance. Our script unfolds as we live. Although much of what happens to us is outside of our control, we do get to choose some things. And how we play our part depends on our perspective on why we are here.

> The Bible reveals to us that our Writer is focused on a plot much greater than we can imagine.

With eyes of faith, we believe our script is part of a bigger story. Our Writer has an objective for our script that our earthly eyes may never see. Through faith, we can rest in the knowledge that the scene we are in, as well as our part in it, serves some purpose in the overall story. And we may be required to personally sacrifice for the good of a storyline we can't see.

The Bible reveals to us that our Writer is focused on a plot much greater than we can imagine. Whether or not we trust that directly affects the way we play our part.

MORE TRUST?

A large group of college students gathered around a wise old woman as she spoke wisdom into their lives. Now in her eighties, she had a wealth of knowledge and experience from a life well lived. They leaned in close, for they wanted to glean from any specific lessons she had learned. Her life had been a testimony to everything they believed and wanted to be.

Growing up in the early 1900s, Henrietta Mears had defied the limitations of a woman in leadership. She influenced some of the most powerful Christian leaders our country ever had. From Billy Graham to Bill Bright, Jim Rayburn to Bob Munger, her influence was felt in books, organizations, and thousands of people who came to believe in the God she talked about and loved.

She also founded the camp where I first heard the news that would change my life.

I was eighteen at the time and in the midst of a three-week romance that illustrated the longevity of my high school relationships. My boyfriend had decided to go to a weekend camp called Forest Home, so naturally I decided to accompany him.

The God described that weekend at Forest Home was different from the one I had heard about growing up. This God didn't just want to be there for emergencies and holidays, he wanted to accompany me in my life. But I learned it was my decision whether I wanted to let this God in. Nervously, I took the plunge and asked a good friend who was already a Christian to stand up with me. Little did I know that decision would completely change the trajectory of my life. Like a compass on a sailboat, that one degree change altered my course.

Forest Home triggered that change. And Henrietta Mears was the woman who founded Forest Home. Years before I stood up to invite God to have my life, she stood in that same place and addressed that group of college students. And at the end of her talk, someone yelled a question that made everyone cringe.

"Miss Mears," the person said, "Now that you are nearing the end of your life, is there anything you would have done differently?"

The awkwardness of asking that kind of question to this great saint silenced the crowd. However, Henrietta Mears wasted no time in answering it. Her eighty-year-old eyes scanned the crowd as she said five simple words: "I would trust God more."

Coming from a woman who lived in such close proximity to this God, her words lay there like a challenge. How would it even be possible to live a life that had more trust than hers? The pastor who recounted the story to me was a college graduate at the time, and he never forgot what she said.

It occurs to me that I've never heard of anyone getting to the end of life only to say, "I wish I hadn't trusted God as much as I did." But if someone like Henrietta Mears proclaims the opposite truth, I for one want to listen. Maybe it will move me to live my life differently and make choices to make the bigger story around me slightly better than it was. That, it appears, is the greatest evidence of a life well lived.

EMBRACING YOUR PART

One could say it was the first recorded episode of *The Bachelor*. It took place in Persia sometime around 485 BC. This story is found in the only book in the Bible that does not mention the name of God. Instead, much like life, God's presence is revealed in the actions and decisions of the people involved in the account.

The narrative begins with a Persian king who has deposed his queen and decides to pull out all the stops to select a new one. Women are brought in from all over the land to be given a chance at winning his heart. After the six months of beauty treatments, each young woman will be brought before the king, and the one who wins his approval will be appointed his wife.

Enter Esther, a Jewish orphan girl, who has been raised by her cousin Mordecai. When she is taken to the palace, her beauty ultimately wins the king's heart. Suddenly this girl is swept from humble beginnings into a much bigger life than she ever imagined hers to be. However, the end of this Cinderella story is only the tip of Esther's life, because *after* she becomes queen, her journey comes to a crossroads. A king's adviser has somehow persuaded the king to sign an edict that would annihilate all Jews, convincing him that their religious customs are a threat to his power. Because Esther was instructed not to tell her origin, the king is unaware his queen is from the group of people he has inadvertently ordered to destroy. When Esther's cousin Mordecai finds out, he tells her that because of her position, she is the only one who can intervene on this decree.

In a dramatic turn of events, Esther suddenly sees all that's happened to her as part of a bigger story. Everything that brought her to this moment is placed into a broader turn of events, and she sees that she is here—at this time—for a purpose much bigger than herself. Her beauty, her triumph, and her position in the palace are now seen from a higher view, as she recognizes that everything may have happened to her for the purpose of touching and affecting other peoples' lives.

As the plot reaches this peak, Mordecai confronts her with the choice that she can remain isolated in her own story or enter into the much bigger story that is taking place around her. In the midst of her decision, she is jolted by her cousin's words: "And who knows but that you have come to your royal position for such a time as this?" (Esther 4:14).

As she is pulled back from the microscope view of her story, Esther suddenly sees her life in a much broader context. She realizes that her decision about how she will move forward carries more weight than she thought. Esther stands at the same crossroads where all of us stand: to either see her life as her own, to do with what she wants, or to see her life as part of God's story, given to her to touch and affect other lives. In Esther's choice, we see a choice that faces us.

Reading on in Jewish history, we see the fruit of her response. She risks her life for the sake of her people, and they are unknowingly saved by her brave act. A Jewish feast called Purim, commemorating the protection and deliverance of the Jews, is still celebrated today, in part because of the courage of this young Jewish queen.

The higher view lens reveals that our stories are given to us for a purpose much bigger than ourselves. But living our part requires great courage when we face chapters of fear and loss. The chapters we would not choose pose the greatest challenge to our trust.

THE GOOD AND THE BAD

When life is good, it's easy to trust the Writer. We grab hold of our script and embrace our current scene. We may hear vague warnings in Scripture to not hold too tightly, that things will change, that we are being prepared for something more, but for one joyous moment we nestle into our happiness. And then the page turns in our script.

The good news is, in difficulty the page also turns, because pages are continually turning as we live our lives. Our challenge is that we don't know from one scene to the next how our story will evolve. But if we trust our Writer, we know the ending is in his hands. God is preparing us for a story much bigger than the one we will live on this earth.

When you look back, you can see some things that appeared to be blessings became great challenges. Relationships or decisions that seemed right at the time are now viewed through a more informed lens. But what is more surprising is that some things you viewed as losses now bring you gratitude. Even endings that brought devastation may have become tempered by seeing the fruit they bore. With the higher view lens, we can step back and realize things are happening *through* our circumstances that we one day will benefit from.

> The bigger story trumps our small story. Keeping that perspective in front of us helps us to embrace each scene.

The bigger story trumps our small story. Keeping that perspective in front of us helps us to embrace each scene. Oddly, in the bigger story the difficult scenes often carry more importance than the easier ones. Because what happens through us in that difficulty may be weightier than we currently see.

A SCRIPT VIEWED IN CONTEXT

One man got a glimpse of his story in the context of the bigger story. As we read his account, we gain insight into how to view our part. When Job initially experiences his loss, he doesn't know what the reader can see—that there was a bigger story happening above him. All he knew was the excruciating pain he endured. Job lost his children, his possessions, and his health, however his own death was the one catastrophe he was not allowed. One day Job was thanking God for giving him life; the next he was crying out to that same God who allowed him to be ravaged with pain. The book of Job documents the fact that he was never given the reason why. What he did get was an encounter with the Writer of his script.

Crying out for an explanation, Job was met with silence. Instead the Writer takes him on a tour so he could see the bigger story. By viewing all that God was capable of, Job gained what the Writer desires from us all: trust.

It is curious that God never told Job the reason he suffered. One can only imagine that if he did, we might demand a reason ourselves. Instead Job is healed by the sheer size of God.

He surrenders his script with these words: "I know that you can do all things; no purpose of yours can be thwarted" (Job 42:2). With new awareness of his limited view, he repents and decides to trust: "Surely I spoke of things I did not understand, things too wonderful for me to know" (Job 42:3).

Job got a glimpse of his story through the higher view lens, but only after he went through more confusion and heartbreak than most of us will ever see. And in spite of the efforts trying to console him and give reasons for his circumstances, only one thing caused him to embrace his script: a shift in perspective.

Is it possible that our attitude about our script would change if we took time each day to shift our perspective?

The truth is, when we give up being the center of our story, we are better able to live it. For our story now stars someone other than ourselves. As supporting players, we can play our roles with the awareness that we are part of God's bigger story, and accept our script as the one we are meant to live.

Simone Weil describes what happens when we experience this shift in perspective: "To give up our imaginary position as the center, to renounce it, not only intellectually but in the imaginative part of our soul, means to awaken to what is real and eternal, to see the true light."

Seeing what is "real and eternal" is the gift the higher view gives us. Like looking through a spiritual lens, it expands what we see. With the higher-view perspective we understand life to be more than our story, our script as being part of a bigger show, and the stage being different than people around us may see. What helps us play our part well is our acceptance of it. With acceptance, we embrace what we might have formerly wished away. With the higher view lens, we realize what is bad might one day be good; things we are tempted to discard might be the most valuable, and everything is working together for good in a way we may not now see.

With trust and acceptance, we come to a place where we can embrace our part. But there is one more thing the higher view gives us, and that is to see the good *in* our part. With gratitude, we find our final secret to seeing our life with new eyes.

THE VISION GRATITUDE GIVES US

If there's one day that reminds us to be grateful, it's Thanksgiving. However, Thanksgiving Day seems to be more diminished by Christmas commercialism every year. I love Christmas, but if department stores have their way, we may completely obliterate the holiday that proceeds it. And we need this holiday for our souls.

In *One Thousand Gifts*, Ann Voskamp writes, "The practice of giving thanks is a way we practice the presence of God, stay present to His presence, and it is always a practice of the eyes. We don't have to change what we see. Only the way we see."

Gratitude doesn't change what we see in front of us; it changes the way we see what we have. However, the day we have set aside to appreciate what we have is gradually diminishing from a full day to a meal to "Let's get done early so we can hit the sales." Better yet, can we just get our turkey to go? Black Friday originally referred to the big sales happening the day after Thanksgiving. However, Black Friday now starts *before* Thanksgiving, and in some homes it supersedes it. People are rushing through giving thanks for what they have so they can stand in line for what they are missing.

I wonder if anyone else sees the irony.

Sarah Ban Breathnach, an author who inspired Ann Voskamp's book, says, "Gratitude bestows reverence, allowing us to encounter everyday epiphanies, those transcendent moments of awe that change forever how we experience life and the world. . . . We discover the sacred in the ordinary and we realize that every day is literally a gift."

Perhaps Thanksgiving is weightier than we think. We need it not only to feed our bodies but to feed our souls. For one day a year our focus is shifted off what is missing and placed instead on what we have. And I fear the shorter the day becomes, the smaller our souls will be. The discipline of giving thanks is the antidote for our wandering eyes.

> The discipline of giving thanks is the antidote for our wandering eyes.

We need this discipline for more than a day a year. An hour a day would be better—or even five minutes a day. The regular practice of thanksgiving shifts our gaze from the things missing to the treasures sitting in front of us—and to take time to appreciate them before they slip away. When they do slip away, we'll recognize how valuable they really are.

How might our life be lived differently if we were able to recognize their value before they were gone?

YOU ARE THE CAMERA

So now, here you are—equipped with the lenses you need in order to see your life with new eyes. However, if you're like me, you may need to be reminded from time to time how to use them. I wrote this book so these stories would help you remember how to put them on. The big view lens will help you continue to see the breadth and power of your life. The present view lens will spur you to focus on all that is around you. The rear view lens will clarify your thoughts and actions, and bring faith for what's ahead. And the higher view lens will expand your vision to all that God wants you to see.

My prayer is that through this book you have begun to see your life differently, and that you now see more beauty and meaning in the story you have been given to live. With your new eyes, I hope you are able to witness more frequently the depth and grandeur and glory that is hidden in every scene of your life.

Carlo Carretto suggests that the presence of God in our life gives us the ability to alter the way we see. Using the example of the way we view the Gospels, he says, "*You are the camera, able to fix inside yourself what you see and what you don't see . . . and the power of fixing an image in the soul depends on the Holy Spirit,* who is love, and who alone is able to make that photograph in proportion to your intimacy with him."

The best way to see life differently is to stay close to the One who gave you your story. For he is also the One who has the power to change your eyes.

With the new perspective God gives you, you are empowered to go back to page one and fill in your own blanks where this book began:

Today I woke up and . . .

From here on out, the rest of this book will be authored by you.

Acknowledgments

Special thanks to

Chris Benedict, Brooke Rundle, Patty Bradley, Audrey Tognotti, Melissa Johnston, Chrissie Velazquez, Susie Peterson, Doug and Laurie Bunnell, Ephraim Lindor, Dennis Wadley, and Erin Beck—your stories breathed life into the lenses of this book.

Gini Bunnell, Vivian McIlraith, and June Michealsen, for your part in shaping my eyes.

Ray Anderson, for introducing me to the "agogic moment," and for using vocabulary that pushed me.

Curt Thompson, for powering my insights on the rear view, and being generous enough to let me interpret them.

John Sloan, who started me on this journey, and let me go with grace into good hands.

Dad, Mom, Tom, Chip, and every Polich, Bliss, and Underhill (before and since) who make up my tribe—you are the family God gave me, and I'm grateful for the support we all have to find our path. I love you more than you know.

Todor Polich (Djedo)—though no longer with us, you left your imprint on us all.

And finally, to Jere and Jordan Short, you are my home.

Notes

INTRODUCTION: THE THINGS YOU MAY NOT SEE

8   *There is enough light*: Blaise Pascal, *Pensées* (New York: Penguin, 1966), 50.

1 THE BIG PICTURE CHANGES THE SMALL PICTURE

30   *The setting was World War II*: Mike Yaconelli, *Messy Spirituality* (Grand Rapids: Zondervan, 2002), 108.

**2 YOUR VIEW OF CIRCUMSTANCES
SHAPES WHAT THEY BECOME**

39   *In 1955*: Martin Luther King Jr., "Looking Beyond Your Circumstances," Dexter Avenue Baptist Church, 1955, Martin Luther King Jr. Papers Project, *Stanford University*, https://kinginstitute .stanford.edu/king-papers/publications/autobiography-martin -luther-king-jr-contents/chapter-6-dexter-avenue.

50   *Whenever we look*: Ibid.

4 SEEING THE PATH IN FRONT OF YOU

70   *Before you tell your life*: Parker Palmer, *Let Your Life Speak* (San Francisco: Jossey-Bass, 2000), 3.

71   *Each time a door*: Ibid., 54.

77   *In 1937, Hubert Mitchell*: This story is adapted from Hubert Mitchell, "The Missionary and the Nail," Billy Graham Center Archives, www2.wheaton.edu/bgc/archives/docs/StoryofaNail /storyofanailtext.htm.

5 SEEING THE PEOPLE ON YOUR PATH

81   *Often characterized as rude*: See Dylan Love, "16 Examples of Steve Jobs Being a Huge Jerk," *Business Insider*, October 25, 2011, www .businessinsider.com/steve-jobs-jerk-2011-10; and Mona Simpson, "A Sister's Eulogy for Steve Jobs," *New York Times*, October 30, 2011, www.nytimes.com/2011/10/30/opinion/mona-simpsons-eulogy -for-steve-jobs.html.

83   *if we are aware*: John Ortberg, *Soul Keeping* (Grand Rapids: Zondervan, 2014), 124.

91   *Vulnerability is*: Brené Brown, *Rising Strong* (New York: Random House, 2015), 4.

91   *It is recorded*: Simpson, "A Sister's Eulogy for Steve Jobs."

6 LOOKING AT YOUR PAST BRINGS CLARITY

97   *In my brief study*: Curt Thompson, *Anatomy of the Soul* (Wheaton, IL: Tyndale House, 2010), 65.

7 LOOKING AT YOUR MEMORIES BUILDS HOPE

112   *when we are remembering*: Curt Thompson, *Anatomy of the Soul* (Wheaton, IL: Tyndale House, 2010), 77.

8 PAUSING TO NOTICE GOD'S GIFTS

121   *It's a great loss*: Ken Gire, *The Reflective Life* (Colorado Springs: Chariot Victor, 1998).

124   *the greatest danger*: Charles E. Hummel, *Tyranny of the Urgent* (Downers Grove, IL: InterVarsity Press, 1967), 5.

131   *God himself works*: Thomas Kelly, *A Testament of Devotion* (New York: Harper & Row, 1941), 41.

9 SEEING THE PURPOSE FOR YOUR PAIN

136   *Making one's own*: Henri Nouwen, *The Wounded Healer* (New York: Image, 1979), 88.

10 OPENING YOUR EYES TO NEED

152   *The less we have*: Jose Luis Gonzalez-Balado, *Mother Teresa: In My Own Words* (New York: Gramercy, 1997).

11: LOOKING AT YOUR LIFE WITH NEW EYES

162   *To give up*: Simone Weil, *Waiting for God* (New York: Harper Perennial Modern Classics, 2009), 100.

164   *The practice of giving*: Ann Voskamp, *One Thousand Gifts* (Grand Rapids: Zondervan, 2010), 135.

164   *Gratitude bestows*: Sarah Ban Breathnach, "Gratitude," *Living Life Fully* (blog), www.livinglifefully.com/flo/flobegratitudesbb.htm

165   *You are the camera*: Carlo Carretto, quoted in *A Guide to Prayer for Ministers and Other Servants* (Nashville: Upper Room, 1983), 24.